THIS JOURNAL BELONGS TO:

_____

INTUITION

WE ALL NATURALLY POSSESS INTUITION, *AND* EVERYONE CAN IMPROVE THEIR INTUITION—IN MANY CASES DRAMATICALLY— SIMPLY THROUGH AWARENESS, UNDERSTANDING, AND PRACTICE.

YOUR RELATIONSHIP WITH THE FOUR INTUITIVE PATHWAYS— CLAIRAUDIENCE (HEARING), CLAIRVOYANCE (SEEING), CLAIR- COGNIZANCE (KNOWING), AND CLAIRSENTIENCE (FEELING)—IS DYNAMIC AND UNIQUELY YOUR OWN. YOU ALREADY HAVE ONE OR MORE INTUITIVE PATHWAYS OPEN AND ACTIVE—EVEN IF YOU DON'T REALIZE IT.

THERE ARE MANY MORE WAYS IN WHICH YOU CAN REGULARLY RECEIVE INTUITIVE GUIDANCE, SUCH AS THROUGH DREAMS, GUT INSTINCTS, OR MEANINGFUL COINCIDENCES. THIS JOURNAL GIVES YOU AMPLE OPPORTUNITY TO ENGAGE WITH AND GROW YOUR SIXTH SENSE.

ARE YOU READY TO AWAKEN YOUR INTUITION?

LEARNING TO CONNECT WITH and recognize the intuitive guidance you receive every day is easier than you might think. Try these steps:

✴ **STAY OPEN AND FLEXIBLE.** Release your attachment to things happening in a certain way, at a certain time, or leading to a certain destination. You get the best from your intuition when you remain open.

✴ **CULTIVATE ENERGY AWARENESS.** Notice energy—your own, the energy of other individuals and groups, the energy of situations and opportunities, the energy of physical spaces, and the fluctuations in world energy.

✴ **QUIET YOUR MIND.** Create more open space between your thoughts to experience fewer thoughts in general. A mind not distracted by mental chatter will more easily recognize intuitive guidance of all kinds.

✴ **SUPPORT YOUR PHYSICAL BODY.** Self-care significantly affects your intuitive abilities. Whether you're healthy, recovering from an injury, or managing a chronic condition, be a protective steward of the vessel that houses your sixth sense.

✴ **BALANCE INTUITION AND PRACTICALITY.** By balancing your sixth-sense guidance with practicality, you create an ideal path forward. Explore how your intuitive insights can be implemented in practical ways.

✴ **REMAIN GROUNDED AND CENTERED.** Observe the world with compassionate curiosity and detachment. Create healthy emotional space between yourself and others.

✴ **VALUE AND VALIDATE YOUR SIXTH SENSE.** Trust that your own intuitive makeup is powerful and yours for a reason. Practice trusting your intuition regarding minor issues to build confidence.

✴ **WORK WITH DIVINATION TOOLS.** Divination tools, like the *Awakening Intuition: Oracle Deck and Guidebook*, can complement your sixth sense. Play with divination tools to enhance or explore your intuition while remembering that *you* are a divination tool!

MORNING REFLECTION

DATE ___/___/___

HOW I'D RATE MY OPENNESS TO INTUITIVE GUIDANCE TODAY:

1   2   3   4   5   6   7   8   9   10

CLOSED/DISTRACTED   OPEN/GROUNDED

LAST NIGHT'S INTUITIVE DREAMS, OR INTUITIVE INSIGHTS WHEN I AWOKE:

_____

_____

TODAY I'D LIKE TO RECEIVE AN INTUITIVE SIGN ABOUT:

_____

_____

GOALS TO HELP ME FEEL LESS SCATTERED AND MORE CENTERED TODAY:

_____   _____

_____   _____

HOW I PLAN TO CONNECT MINDFULLY WITH MY INTUITION TODAY:

_____

_____

_____

MY MORNING INTUITIVE ROUTINE INCLUDED:

☐ MEDITATION   ☐ TIME IN NATURE   ☐ SELF-CARE:_____

☐ PRAYER   ☐ A HEALTHY BREAKFAST   ☐ OTHER:_____

☐ JOURNALING   ☐ SACRED PAUSES   _____

GUT CHECK—WHAT IS THE STRONGEST INSTINCT I HAVE RIGHT NOW ABOUT
HOW TO APPROACH A SITUATION, PERSON, OR ISSUE I'M FACING TODAY?

_____

_____

EVENING REFLECTION

HOW I'D RATE MY ABILITY TO CONNECT WITH MY INTUITION TODAY:

1   2   3   4   5   6   7   8   9   10

DISCONNECTED   CONNECTED

MEANINGFUL COINCIDENCES, THEMES, OR PATTERNS I ENCOUNTERED TODAY:

_____

_____

_____

INTUITIVE INSIGHTS I EXPERIENCED INTERNALLY OR PHYSICALLY:

_____

_____

THINGS THAT CONNECTED ME TO MY INTUITION TODAY:

- [ ] GETTING QUALITY QUIET TIME OR TIME ALONE
- [ ] MINDFULLY SLOWING DOWN
- [ ] LOWERING MY STRESS LEVELS
- [ ] HAVING NOURISHING WORK AND HOME ROUTINES
- [ ] KEEPING MY ENVIRONMENT TIDY AND INVITING
- [ ] LISTENING TO SOFT MUSIC OR NATURE SOUNDS
- [ ] PULLING AN ORACLE CARD FOR INSPIRATION
- [ ] OTHER: _____

WHERE/WHEN DID I FEEL MOST INTUITIVE TODAY?

_____

_____

WHAT WAS MOST ENCOURAGING, COMFORTING, OR EXCITING ABOUT CONNECTING WITH MY INTUITION TODAY?

_____

_____

MORNING REFLECTION

DATE ___ / ___ / ___

HOW I'D RATE MY OPENNESS TO INTUITIVE GUIDANCE TODAY:

1   2   3   4   5   6   7   8   9   10

CLOSED/DISTRACTED   OPEN/GROUNDED

LAST NIGHT'S INTUITIVE DREAMS, OR INTUITIVE INSIGHTS WHEN I AWOKE:

_____

_____

TODAY I'D LIKE TO RECEIVE AN INTUITIVE SIGN ABOUT:

_____

_____

GOALS TO HELP ME FEEL LESS SCATTERED AND MORE CENTERED TODAY:

_____   _____

_____   _____

HOW I PLAN TO CONNECT MINDFULLY WITH MY INTUITION TODAY:

_____

_____

_____

MY MORNING INTUITIVE ROUTINE INCLUDED:

- ☐ MEDITATION
- ☐ PRAYER
- ☐ JOURNALING

- ☐ TIME IN NATURE
- ☐ A HEALTHY BREAKFAST
- ☐ SACRED PAUSES

- ☐ SELF-CARE:_____
- ☐ OTHER:_____
- _____

GUT CHECK—WHAT IS THE STRONGEST INSTINCT I HAVE RIGHT NOW ABOUT HOW TO APPROACH A SITUATION, PERSON, OR ISSUE I'M FACING TODAY?

_____

_____

_____

EVENING REFLECTION

HOW I'D RATE MY ABILITY TO CONNECT WITH MY INTUITION TODAY:

1   2   3   4   5   6   7   8   9   10

DISCONNECTED   CONNECTED

MEANINGFUL COINCIDENCES, THEMES, OR PATTERNS I ENCOUNTERED TODAY:

_____

_____

_____

INTUITIVE INSIGHTS I EXPERIENCED INTERNALLY OR PHYSICALLY:

_____

_____

THINGS THAT CONNECTED ME TO MY INTUITION TODAY:

☐ GETTING QUALITY QUIET TIME OR TIME ALONE

☐ MINDFULLY SLOWING DOWN

☐ LOWERING MY STRESS LEVELS

☐ HAVING NOURISHING WORK AND HOME ROUTINES

☐ KEEPING MY ENVIRONMENT TIDY AND INVITING

☐ LISTENING TO SOFT MUSIC OR NATURE SOUNDS

☐ PULLING AN ORACLE CARD FOR INSPIRATION

☐ OTHER:_____

WHERE/WHEN DID I FEEL MOST INTUITIVE TODAY?

_____

_____

WHAT WAS MOST ENCOURAGING, COMFORTING, OR EXCITING ABOUT
CONNECTING WITH MY INTUITION TODAY?

_____

_____

MORNING REFLECTION   DATE ___/___/___

HOW I'D RATE MY OPENNESS TO INTUITIVE GUIDANCE TODAY:

1   2   3   4   5   6   7   8   9   10

CLOSED/DISTRACTED   OPEN/GROUNDED

LAST NIGHT'S INTUITIVE DREAMS, OR INTUITIVE INSIGHTS WHEN I AWOKE:
_____

_____

TODAY I'D LIKE TO RECEIVE AN INTUITIVE SIGN ABOUT:
_____

_____

GOALS TO HELP ME FEEL LESS SCATTERED AND MORE CENTERED TODAY:
_____   _____

_____   _____

HOW I PLAN TO CONNECT MINDFULLY WITH MY INTUITION TODAY:
_____

_____

_____

MY MORNING INTUITIVE ROUTINE INCLUDED:

☐ MEDITATION   ☐ TIME IN NATURE   ☐ SELF-CARE:_____

☐ PRAYER   ☐ A HEALTHY BREAKFAST   ☐ OTHER:_____

☐ JOURNALING   ☐ SACRED PAUSES   _____

GUT CHECK—WHAT IS THE STRONGEST INSTINCT I HAVE RIGHT NOW ABOUT
HOW TO APPROACH A SITUATION, PERSON, OR ISSUE I'M FACING TODAY?
_____

_____

_____

EVENING REFLECTION

HOW I'D RATE MY ABILITY TO CONNECT WITH MY INTUITION TODAY:

1	2	3	4	5	6	7	8	9	10

DISCONNECTED   CONNECTED

MEANINGFUL COINCIDENCES, THEMES, OR PATTERNS I ENCOUNTERED TODAY:

_____

_____

_____

INTUITIVE INSIGHTS I EXPERIENCED INTERNALLY OR PHYSICALLY:

_____

_____

THINGS THAT CONNECTED ME TO MY INTUITION TODAY:

- [ ] GETTING QUALITY QUIET TIME OR TIME ALONE
- [ ] MINDFULLY SLOWING DOWN
- [ ] LOWERING MY STRESS LEVELS
- [ ] HAVING NOURISHING WORK AND HOME ROUTINES
- [ ] KEEPING MY ENVIRONMENT TIDY AND INVITING
- [ ] LISTENING TO SOFT MUSIC OR NATURE SOUNDS
- [ ] PULLING AN ORACLE CARD FOR INSPIRATION
- [ ] OTHER:_____

WHERE/WHEN DID I FEEL MOST INTUITIVE TODAY?

_____

_____

WHAT WAS MOST ENCOURAGING, COMFORTING, OR EXCITING ABOUT
CONNECTING WITH MY INTUITION TODAY?

_____

_____

MORNING REFLECTION

DATE ___/___/___

HOW I'D RATE MY OPENNESS TO INTUITIVE GUIDANCE TODAY:

1   2   3   4   5   6   7   8   9   10

CLOSED/DISTRACTED   OPEN/GROUNDED

LAST NIGHT'S INTUITIVE DREAMS, OR INTUITIVE INSIGHTS WHEN I AWOKE:

_____

_____

TODAY I'D LIKE TO RECEIVE AN INTUITIVE SIGN ABOUT:

_____

_____

GOALS TO HELP ME FEEL LESS SCATTERED AND MORE CENTERED TODAY:

_____   _____

_____   _____

HOW I PLAN TO CONNECT MINDFULLY WITH MY INTUITION TODAY:

_____

_____

_____

MY MORNING INTUITIVE ROUTINE INCLUDED:

☐ MEDITATION   ☐ TIME IN NATURE   ☐ SELF-CARE:_____

☐ PRAYER   ☐ A HEALTHY BREAKFAST   ☐ OTHER:_____

☐ JOURNALING   ☐ SACRED PAUSES   _____

GUT CHECK—WHAT IS THE STRONGEST INSTINCT I HAVE RIGHT NOW ABOUT
HOW TO APPROACH A SITUATION, PERSON, OR ISSUE I'M FACING TODAY?

_____

_____

EVENING REFLECTION

HOW I'D RATE MY ABILITY TO CONNECT WITH MY INTUITION TODAY:

1	2	3	4	5	6	7	8	9	10

DISCONNECTED   CONNECTED

MEANINGFUL COINCIDENCES, THEMES, OR PATTERNS I ENCOUNTERED TODAY:

_____

_____

_____

INTUITIVE INSIGHTS I EXPERIENCED INTERNALLY OR PHYSICALLY:

_____

_____

THINGS THAT CONNECTED ME TO MY INTUITION TODAY:

☐ GETTING QUALITY QUIET TIME OR TIME ALONE

☐ MINDFULLY SLOWING DOWN

☐ LOWERING MY STRESS LEVELS

☐ HAVING NOURISHING WORK AND HOME ROUTINES

☐ KEEPING MY ENVIRONMENT TIDY AND INVITING

☐ LISTENING TO SOFT MUSIC OR NATURE SOUNDS

☐ PULLING AN ORACLE CARD FOR INSPIRATION

☐ OTHER:_____

WHERE/WHEN DID I FEEL MOST INTUITIVE TODAY?

_____

_____

WHAT WAS MOST ENCOURAGING, COMFORTING, OR EXCITING ABOUT
CONNECTING WITH MY INTUITION TODAY?

_____

_____

MORNING REFLECTION DATE ___/___/___

HOW I'D RATE MY OPENNESS TO INTUITIVE GUIDANCE TODAY:

1   2   3   4   5   6   7   8   9   10

CLOSED/DISTRACTED   OPEN/GROUNDED

LAST NIGHT'S INTUITIVE DREAMS, OR INTUITIVE INSIGHTS WHEN I AWOKE:

_____

_____

TODAY I'D LIKE TO RECEIVE AN INTUITIVE SIGN ABOUT:

_____

_____

GOALS TO HELP ME FEEL LESS SCATTERED AND MORE CENTERED TODAY:

_____   _____

_____   _____

HOW I PLAN TO CONNECT MINDFULLY WITH MY INTUITION TODAY:

_____

_____

_____

MY MORNING INTUITIVE ROUTINE INCLUDED:

☐ MEDITATION   ☐ TIME IN NATURE   ☐ SELF-CARE:_____

☐ PRAYER   ☐ A HEALTHY BREAKFAST   ☐ OTHER:_____

☐ JOURNALING   ☐ SACRED PAUSES   _____

GUT CHECK—WHAT IS THE STRONGEST INSTINCT I HAVE RIGHT NOW ABOUT
HOW TO APPROACH A SITUATION, PERSON, OR ISSUE I'M FACING TODAY?

_____

_____

_____

EVENING REFLECTION

HOW I'D RATE MY ABILITY TO CONNECT WITH MY INTUITION TODAY:

1   2   3   4   5   6   7   8   9   10

DISCONNECTED   CONNECTED

MEANINGFUL COINCIDENCES, THEMES, OR PATTERNS I ENCOUNTERED TODAY:

_____

_____

_____

INTUITIVE INSIGHTS I EXPERIENCED INTERNALLY OR PHYSICALLY:

_____

_____

THINGS THAT CONNECTED ME TO MY INTUITION TODAY:

- [ ] GETTING QUALITY QUIET TIME OR TIME ALONE
- [ ] MINDFULLY SLOWING DOWN
- [ ] LOWERING MY STRESS LEVELS
- [ ] HAVING NOURISHING WORK AND HOME ROUTINES
- [ ] KEEPING MY ENVIRONMENT TIDY AND INVITING
- [ ] LISTENING TO SOFT MUSIC OR NATURE SOUNDS
- [ ] PULLING AN ORACLE CARD FOR INSPIRATION
- [ ] OTHER:_____

WHERE/WHEN DID I FEEL MOST INTUITIVE TODAY?

_____

_____

WHAT WAS MOST ENCOURAGING, COMFORTING, OR EXCITING ABOUT
CONNECTING WITH MY INTUITION TODAY?

_____

_____

MORNING REFLECTION   DATE ___/___/___

LAST NIGHT'S INTUITIVE DREAMS, OR INTUITIVE INSIGHTS WHEN I AWOKE:

_____

_____

TODAY I'D LIKE TO RECEIVE AN INTUITIVE SIGN ABOUT:

_____

_____

GOALS TO HELP ME FEEL LESS SCATTERED AND MORE CENTERED TODAY:

_____   _____

_____   _____

HOW I PLAN TO CONNECT MINDFULLY WITH MY INTUITION TODAY:

_____

_____

_____

MY MORNING INTUITIVE ROUTINE INCLUDED:

☐ MEDITATION   ☐ TIME IN NATURE   ☐ SELF-CARE:_____

☐ PRAYER   ☐ A HEALTHY BREAKFAST   ☐ OTHER:_____

☐ JOURNALING   ☐ SACRED PAUSES   _____

GUT CHECK—WHAT IS THE STRONGEST INSTINCT I HAVE RIGHT NOW ABOUT
HOW TO APPROACH A SITUATION, PERSON, OR ISSUE I'M FACING TODAY?

_____

_____

_____

EVENING REFLECTION

HOW I'D RATE MY ABILITY TO CONNECT WITH MY INTUITION TODAY:

| 1 | 2 | 3 | 4 | 5 | 6 | 7 | 8 | 9 | 10 |

DISCONNECTED   CONNECTED

MEANINGFUL COINCIDENCES, THEMES, OR PATTERNS I ENCOUNTERED TODAY:
_____
_____
_____

INTUITIVE INSIGHTS I EXPERIENCED INTERNALLY OR PHYSICALLY:
_____
_____

THINGS THAT CONNECTED ME TO MY INTUITION TODAY:

- [ ] GETTING QUALITY QUIET TIME OR TIME ALONE
- [ ] MINDFULLY SLOWING DOWN
- [ ] LOWERING MY STRESS LEVELS
- [ ] HAVING NOURISHING WORK AND HOME ROUTINES
- [ ] KEEPING MY ENVIRONMENT TIDY AND INVITING
- [ ] LISTENING TO SOFT MUSIC OR NATURE SOUNDS
- [ ] PULLING AN ORACLE CARD FOR INSPIRATION
- [ ] OTHER:_____

WHERE/WHEN DID I FEEL MOST INTUITIVE TODAY?
_____
_____

WHAT WAS MOST ENCOURAGING, COMFORTING, OR EXCITING ABOUT
CONNECTING WITH MY INTUITION TODAY?
_____
_____

MORNING REFLECTION

DATE ___/___/___

HOW I'D RATE MY OPENNESS TO INTUITIVE GUIDANCE TODAY:

1   2   3   4   5   6   7   8   9   10

CLOSED/DISTRACTED   OPEN/GROUNDED

LAST NIGHT'S INTUITIVE DREAMS, OR INTUITIVE INSIGHTS WHEN I AWOKE:

_____

_____

TODAY I'D LIKE TO RECEIVE AN INTUITIVE SIGN ABOUT:

_____

_____

GOALS TO HELP ME FEEL LESS SCATTERED AND MORE CENTERED TODAY:

_____   _____

_____   _____

HOW I PLAN TO CONNECT MINDFULLY WITH MY INTUITION TODAY:

_____

_____

_____

MY MORNING INTUITIVE ROUTINE INCLUDED:

☐ MEDITATION   ☐ TIME IN NATURE   ☐ SELF-CARE:_____

☐ PRAYER   ☐ A HEALTHY BREAKFAST   ☐ OTHER:_____

☐ JOURNALING   ☐ SACRED PAUSES   _____

GUT CHECK—WHAT IS THE STRONGEST INSTINCT I HAVE RIGHT NOW ABOUT
HOW TO APPROACH A SITUATION, PERSON, OR ISSUE I'M FACING TODAY?

_____

_____

_____

EVENING REFLECTION

HOW I'D RATE MY ABILITY TO CONNECT WITH MY INTUITION TODAY:

1   2   3   4   5   6   7   8   9   10

DISCONNECTED   CONNECTED

MEANINGFUL COINCIDENCES, THEMES, OR PATTERNS I ENCOUNTERED TODAY:

_____

_____

_____

INTUITIVE INSIGHTS I EXPERIENCED INTERNALLY OR PHYSICALLY:

_____

_____

THINGS THAT CONNECTED ME TO MY INTUITION TODAY:

☐ GETTING QUALITY QUIET TIME OR TIME ALONE

☐ MINDFULLY SLOWING DOWN

☐ LOWERING MY STRESS LEVELS

☐ HAVING NOURISHING WORK AND HOME ROUTINES

☐ KEEPING MY ENVIRONMENT TIDY AND INVITING

☐ LISTENING TO SOFT MUSIC OR NATURE SOUNDS

☐ PULLING AN ORACLE CARD FOR INSPIRATION

☐ OTHER:_____

WHERE/WHEN DID I FEEL MOST INTUITIVE TODAY?

_____

_____

WHAT WAS MOST ENCOURAGING, COMFORTING, OR EXCITING ABOUT
CONNECTING WITH MY INTUITION TODAY?

_____

_____

MORNING REFLECTION

DATE ___/___/___

HOW I'D RATE MY OPENNESS TO INTUITIVE GUIDANCE TODAY:

1   2   3   4   5   6   7   8   9   10

CLOSED/DISTRACTED   OPEN/GROUNDED

LAST NIGHT'S INTUITIVE DREAMS, OR INTUITIVE INSIGHTS WHEN I AWOKE:

_____

_____

TODAY I'D LIKE TO RECEIVE AN INTUITIVE SIGN ABOUT:

_____

_____

GOALS TO HELP ME FEEL LESS SCATTERED AND MORE CENTERED TODAY:

_____   _____

_____   _____

HOW I PLAN TO CONNECT MINDFULLY WITH MY INTUITION TODAY:

_____

_____

_____

MY MORNING INTUITIVE ROUTINE INCLUDED:

☐ MEDITATION   ☐ TIME IN NATURE   ☐ SELF-CARE:_____

☐ PRAYER   ☐ A HEALTHY BREAKFAST   ☐ OTHER:_____

☐ JOURNALING   ☐ SACRED PAUSES   _____

GUT CHECK—WHAT IS THE STRONGEST INSTINCT I HAVE RIGHT NOW ABOUT
HOW TO APPROACH A SITUATION, PERSON, OR ISSUE I'M FACING TODAY?

_____

_____

_____

EVENING REFLECTION

HOW I'D RATE MY ABILITY TO CONNECT WITH MY INTUITION TODAY:

1   2   3   4   5   6   7   8   9   10

DISCONNECTED   CONNECTED

MEANINGFUL COINCIDENCES, THEMES, OR PATTERNS I ENCOUNTERED TODAY:

_____

_____

_____

INTUITIVE INSIGHTS I EXPERIENCED INTERNALLY OR PHYSICALLY:

_____

_____

THINGS THAT CONNECTED ME TO MY INTUITION TODAY:

☐ GETTING QUALITY QUIET TIME OR TIME ALONE

☐ MINDFULLY SLOWING DOWN

☐ LOWERING MY STRESS LEVELS

☐ HAVING NOURISHING WORK AND HOME ROUTINES

☐ KEEPING MY ENVIRONMENT TIDY AND INVITING

☐ LISTENING TO SOFT MUSIC OR NATURE SOUNDS

☐ PULLING AN ORACLE CARD FOR INSPIRATION

☐ OTHER:_____

WHERE/WHEN DID I FEEL MOST INTUITIVE TODAY?

_____

_____

WHAT WAS MOST ENCOURAGING, COMFORTING, OR EXCITING ABOUT
CONNECTING WITH MY INTUITION TODAY?

_____

_____

MORNING REFLECTION

DATE ___/___/___

HOW I'D RATE MY OPENNESS TO INTUITIVE GUIDANCE TODAY:

1   2   3   4   5   6   7   8   9   10

CLOSED/DISTRACTED   OPEN/GROUNDED

LAST NIGHT'S INTUITIVE DREAMS, OR INTUITIVE INSIGHTS WHEN I AWOKE:

_____

_____

TODAY I'D LIKE TO RECEIVE AN INTUITIVE SIGN ABOUT:

_____

_____

GOALS TO HELP ME FEEL LESS SCATTERED AND MORE CENTERED TODAY:

_____   _____

_____   _____

HOW I PLAN TO CONNECT MINDFULLY WITH MY INTUITION TODAY:

_____

_____

_____

MY MORNING INTUITIVE ROUTINE INCLUDED:

☐ MEDITATION   ☐ TIME IN NATURE   ☐ SELF-CARE:_____

☐ PRAYER   ☐ A HEALTHY BREAKFAST   ☐ OTHER:_____

☐ JOURNALING   ☐ SACRED PAUSES   _____

GUT CHECK—WHAT IS THE STRONGEST INSTINCT I HAVE RIGHT NOW ABOUT
HOW TO APPROACH A SITUATION, PERSON, OR ISSUE I'M FACING TODAY?

_____

_____

_____

EVENING REFLECTION

MEANINGFUL COINCIDENCES, THEMES, OR PATTERNS I ENCOUNTERED TODAY:

_____

_____

_____

INTUITIVE INSIGHTS I EXPERIENCED INTERNALLY OR PHYSICALLY:

_____

_____

THINGS THAT CONNECTED ME TO MY INTUITION TODAY:

☐ GETTING QUALITY QUIET TIME OR TIME ALONE

☐ MINDFULLY SLOWING DOWN

☐ LOWERING MY STRESS LEVELS

☐ HAVING NOURISHING WORK AND HOME ROUTINES

☐ KEEPING MY ENVIRONMENT TIDY AND INVITING

☐ LISTENING TO SOFT MUSIC OR NATURE SOUNDS

☐ PULLING AN ORACLE CARD FOR INSPIRATION

☐ OTHER:_____

WHERE/WHEN DID I FEEL MOST INTUITIVE TODAY?

_____

_____

WHAT WAS MOST ENCOURAGING, COMFORTING, OR EXCITING ABOUT
CONNECTING WITH MY INTUITION TODAY?

_____

_____

MORNING REFLECTION

DATE ___/___/___

HOW I'D RATE MY OPENNESS TO INTUITIVE GUIDANCE TODAY:

1   2   3   4   5   6   7   8   9   10

CLOSED/DISTRACTED   OPEN/GROUNDED

LAST NIGHT'S INTUITIVE DREAMS, OR INTUITIVE INSIGHTS WHEN I AWOKE:
_____
_____

TODAY I'D LIKE TO RECEIVE AN INTUITIVE SIGN ABOUT:
_____
_____

GOALS TO HELP ME FEEL LESS SCATTERED AND MORE CENTERED TODAY:
_____   _____
_____   _____

HOW I PLAN TO CONNECT MINDFULLY WITH MY INTUITION TODAY:
_____
_____
_____

MY MORNING INTUITIVE ROUTINE INCLUDED:

☐ MEDITATION   ☐ TIME IN NATURE   ☐ SELF-CARE:_____

☐ PRAYER   ☐ A HEALTHY BREAKFAST   ☐ OTHER:_____

☐ JOURNALING   ☐ SACRED PAUSES   _____

GUT CHECK—WHAT IS THE STRONGEST INSTINCT I HAVE RIGHT NOW ABOUT
HOW TO APPROACH A SITUATION, PERSON, OR ISSUE I'M FACING TODAY?
_____
_____
_____

EVENING REFLECTION

MEANINGFUL COINCIDENCES, THEMES, OR PATTERNS I ENCOUNTERED TODAY:

_____

_____

_____

INTUITIVE INSIGHTS I EXPERIENCED INTERNALLY OR PHYSICALLY:

_____

_____

THINGS THAT CONNECTED ME TO MY INTUITION TODAY:

☐ GETTING QUALITY QUIET TIME OR TIME ALONE

☐ MINDFULLY SLOWING DOWN

☐ LOWERING MY STRESS LEVELS

☐ HAVING NOURISHING WORK AND HOME ROUTINES

☐ KEEPING MY ENVIRONMENT TIDY AND INVITING

☐ LISTENING TO SOFT MUSIC OR NATURE SOUNDS

☐ PULLING AN ORACLE CARD FOR INSPIRATION

☐ OTHER:_____

WHERE/WHEN DID I FEEL MOST INTUITIVE TODAY?

_____

_____

WHAT WAS MOST ENCOURAGING, COMFORTING, OR EXCITING ABOUT
CONNECTING WITH MY INTUITION TODAY?

_____

_____

MORNING REFLECTION DATE ___/___/___

LAST NIGHT'S INTUITIVE DREAMS, OR INTUITIVE INSIGHTS WHEN I AWOKE:
_____
_____

TODAY I'D LIKE TO RECEIVE AN INTUITIVE SIGN ABOUT:
_____
_____

GOALS TO HELP ME FEEL LESS SCATTERED AND MORE CENTERED TODAY:
_____   _____
_____   _____

HOW I PLAN TO CONNECT MINDFULLY WITH MY INTUITION TODAY:
_____
_____
_____

MY MORNING INTUITIVE ROUTINE INCLUDED:

☐ MEDITATION   ☐ TIME IN NATURE   ☐ SELF-CARE:_____
☐ PRAYER   ☐ A HEALTHY BREAKFAST   ☐ OTHER:_____
☐ JOURNALING   ☐ SACRED PAUSES   _____

GUT CHECK—WHAT IS THE STRONGEST INSTINCT I HAVE RIGHT NOW ABOUT
HOW TO APPROACH A SITUATION, PERSON, OR ISSUE I'M FACING TODAY?
_____
_____
_____

EVENING REFLECTION

HOW I'D RATE MY ABILITY TO CONNECT WITH MY INTUITION TODAY:

1	2	3	4	5	6	7	8	9	10

DISCONNECTED   CONNECTED

MEANINGFUL COINCIDENCES, THEMES, OR PATTERNS I ENCOUNTERED TODAY:
_____
_____
_____

INTUITIVE INSIGHTS I EXPERIENCED INTERNALLY OR PHYSICALLY:
_____
_____

THINGS THAT CONNECTED ME TO MY INTUITION TODAY:

☐ GETTING QUALITY QUIET TIME OR TIME ALONE
☐ MINDFULLY SLOWING DOWN
☐ LOWERING MY STRESS LEVELS
☐ HAVING NOURISHING WORK AND HOME ROUTINES
☐ KEEPING MY ENVIRONMENT TIDY AND INVITING
☐ LISTENING TO SOFT MUSIC OR NATURE SOUNDS
☐ PULLING AN ORACLE CARD FOR INSPIRATION
☐ OTHER:_____

WHERE/WHEN DID I FEEL MOST INTUITIVE TODAY?
_____
_____

WHAT WAS MOST ENCOURAGING, COMFORTING, OR EXCITING ABOUT
CONNECTING WITH MY INTUITION TODAY?
_____
_____

MORNING REFLECTION

DATE ___/___/___

HOW I'D RATE MY OPENNESS TO INTUITIVE GUIDANCE TODAY:

1   2   3   4   5   6   7   8   9   10

CLOSED/DISTRACTED   OPEN/GROUNDED

LAST NIGHT'S INTUITIVE DREAMS, OR INTUITIVE INSIGHTS WHEN I AWOKE:

_____

_____

TODAY I'D LIKE TO RECEIVE AN INTUITIVE SIGN ABOUT:

_____

_____

GOALS TO HELP ME FEEL LESS SCATTERED AND MORE CENTERED TODAY:

_____   _____

_____   _____

HOW I PLAN TO CONNECT MINDFULLY WITH MY INTUITION TODAY:

_____

_____

_____

MY MORNING INTUITIVE ROUTINE INCLUDED:

☐ MEDITATION   ☐ TIME IN NATURE   ☐ SELF-CARE:_____

☐ PRAYER   ☐ A HEALTHY BREAKFAST   ☐ OTHER:_____

☐ JOURNALING   ☐ SACRED PAUSES   _____

GUT CHECK—WHAT IS THE STRONGEST INSTINCT I HAVE RIGHT NOW ABOUT
HOW TO APPROACH A SITUATION, PERSON, OR ISSUE I'M FACING TODAY?

_____

_____

_____

EVENING REFLECTION

HOW I'D RATE MY ABILITY TO CONNECT WITH MY INTUITION TODAY:

| 1 | 2 | 3 | 4 | 5 | 6 | 7 | 8 | 9 | 10 |

DISCONNECTED   CONNECTED

MEANINGFUL COINCIDENCES, THEMES, OR PATTERNS I ENCOUNTERED TODAY:

_____

_____

_____

INTUITIVE INSIGHTS I EXPERIENCED INTERNALLY OR PHYSICALLY:

_____

_____

THINGS THAT CONNECTED ME TO MY INTUITION TODAY:

☐ GETTING QUALITY QUIET TIME OR TIME ALONE

☐ MINDFULLY SLOWING DOWN

☐ LOWERING MY STRESS LEVELS

☐ HAVING NOURISHING WORK AND HOME ROUTINES

☐ KEEPING MY ENVIRONMENT TIDY AND INVITING

☐ LISTENING TO SOFT MUSIC OR NATURE SOUNDS

☐ PULLING AN ORACLE CARD FOR INSPIRATION

☐ OTHER:_____

WHERE/WHEN DID I FEEL MOST INTUITIVE TODAY?

_____

_____

WHAT WAS MOST ENCOURAGING, COMFORTING, OR EXCITING ABOUT
CONNECTING WITH MY INTUITION TODAY?

_____

_____

MORNING REFLECTION

DATE ___/___/___

HOW I'D RATE MY OPENNESS TO INTUITIVE GUIDANCE TODAY:

1   2   3   4   5   6   7   8   9   10

CLOSED/DISTRACTED   OPEN/GROUNDED

LAST NIGHT'S INTUITIVE DREAMS, OR INTUITIVE INSIGHTS WHEN I AWOKE:

_____

_____

TODAY I'D LIKE TO RECEIVE AN INTUITIVE SIGN ABOUT:

_____

_____

GOALS TO HELP ME FEEL LESS SCATTERED AND MORE CENTERED TODAY:

_____   _____

_____   _____

HOW I PLAN TO CONNECT MINDFULLY WITH MY INTUITION TODAY:

_____

_____

_____

MY MORNING INTUITIVE ROUTINE INCLUDED:

☐ MEDITATION   ☐ TIME IN NATURE   ☐ SELF-CARE:_____

☐ PRAYER   ☐ A HEALTHY BREAKFAST   ☐ OTHER:_____

☐ JOURNALING   ☐ SACRED PAUSES   _____

GUT CHECK—WHAT IS THE STRONGEST INSTINCT I HAVE RIGHT NOW ABOUT
HOW TO APPROACH A SITUATION, PERSON, OR ISSUE I'M FACING TODAY?

_____

_____

_____

EVENING REFLECTION

HOW I'D RATE MY ABILITY TO CONNECT WITH MY INTUITION TODAY:

1	2	3	4	5	6	7	8	9	10

DISCONNECTED·   CONNECTED·

MEANINGFUL COINCIDENCES, THEMES, OR PATTERNS I ENCOUNTERED TODAY:

_____

_____

_____

INTUITIVE INSIGHTS I EXPERIENCED INTERNALLY OR PHYSICALLY:

_____

_____

THINGS THAT CONNECTED ME TO MY INTUITION TODAY:

☐ GETTING QUALITY QUIET TIME OR TIME ALONE

☐ MINDFULLY SLOWING DOWN

☐ LOWERING MY STRESS LEVELS

☐ HAVING NOURISHING WORK AND HOME ROUTINES

☐ KEEPING MY ENVIRONMENT TIDY AND INVITING

☐ LISTENING TO SOFT MUSIC OR NATURE SOUNDS

☐ PULLING AN ORACLE CARD FOR INSPIRATION

☐ OTHER:_____

WHERE/WHEN DID I FEEL MOST INTUITIVE TODAY?

_____

_____

WHAT WAS MOST ENCOURAGING, COMFORTING, OR EXCITING ABOUT
CONNECTING WITH MY INTUITION TODAY?

_____

_____

MORNING REFLECTION
DATE ___/___/___

HOW I'D RATE MY OPENNESS TO INTUITIVE GUIDANCE TODAY:

1   2   3   4   5   6   7   8   9   10

CLOSED/DISTRACTED   OPEN/GROUNDED

LAST NIGHT'S INTUITIVE DREAMS, OR INTUITIVE INSIGHTS WHEN I AWOKE:

_____

_____

TODAY I'D LIKE TO RECEIVE AN INTUITIVE SIGN ABOUT:

_____

_____

GOALS TO HELP ME FEEL LESS SCATTERED AND MORE CENTERED TODAY:

_____   _____

_____   _____

HOW I PLAN TO CONNECT MINDFULLY WITH MY INTUITION TODAY:

_____

_____

_____

MY MORNING INTUITIVE ROUTINE INCLUDED:

☐ MEDITATION   ☐ TIME IN NATURE   ☐ SELF-CARE:_____

☐ PRAYER   ☐ A HEALTHY BREAKFAST   ☐ OTHER:_____

☐ JOURNALING   ☐ SACRED PAUSES   _____

GUT CHECK—WHAT IS THE STRONGEST INSTINCT I HAVE RIGHT NOW ABOUT
HOW TO APPROACH A SITUATION, PERSON, OR ISSUE I'M FACING TODAY?

_____

_____

_____

EVENING REFLECTION

HOW I'D RATE MY ABILITY TO CONNECT WITH MY INTUITION TODAY:

1	2	3	4	5	6	7	8	9	10

DISCONNECTED   CONNECTED

MEANINGFUL COINCIDENCES, THEMES, OR PATTERNS I ENCOUNTERED TODAY:

_____

_____

_____

INTUITIVE INSIGHTS I EXPERIENCED INTERNALLY OR PHYSICALLY:

_____

_____

THINGS THAT CONNECTED ME TO MY INTUITION TODAY:

- [ ] GETTING QUALITY QUIET TIME OR TIME ALONE
- [ ] MINDFULLY SLOWING DOWN
- [ ] LOWERING MY STRESS LEVELS
- [ ] HAVING NOURISHING WORK AND HOME ROUTINES
- [ ] KEEPING MY ENVIRONMENT TIDY AND INVITING
- [ ] LISTENING TO SOFT MUSIC OR NATURE SOUNDS
- [ ] PULLING AN ORACLE CARD FOR INSPIRATION
- [ ] OTHER:_____

WHERE/WHEN DID I FEEL MOST INTUITIVE TODAY?

_____

_____

WHAT WAS MOST ENCOURAGING, COMFORTING, OR EXCITING ABOUT
CONNECTING WITH MY INTUITION TODAY?

_____

_____

MORNING REFLECTION   DATE ___/___/___

HOW I'D RATE MY OPENNESS TO INTUITIVE GUIDANCE TODAY:

1   2   3   4   5   6   7   8   9   10

CLOSED/DISTRACTED   OPEN/GROUNDED

LAST NIGHT'S INTUITIVE DREAMS, OR INTUITIVE INSIGHTS WHEN I AWOKE:

_____

_____

TODAY I'D LIKE TO RECEIVE AN INTUITIVE SIGN ABOUT:

_____

_____

GOALS TO HELP ME FEEL LESS SCATTERED AND MORE CENTERED TODAY:

_____   _____

_____   _____

HOW I PLAN TO CONNECT MINDFULLY WITH MY INTUITION TODAY:

_____

_____

_____

MY MORNING INTUITIVE ROUTINE INCLUDED:

☐ MEDITATION   ☐ TIME IN NATURE   ☐ SELF-CARE:_____

☐ PRAYER   ☐ A HEALTHY BREAKFAST   ☐ OTHER:_____

☐ JOURNALING   ☐ SACRED PAUSES   _____

GUT CHECK—WHAT IS THE STRONGEST INSTINCT I HAVE RIGHT NOW ABOUT
HOW TO APPROACH A SITUATION, PERSON, OR ISSUE I'M FACING TODAY?

_____

_____

_____

EVENING REFLECTION

HOW I'D RATE MY ABILITY TO CONNECT WITH MY INTUITION TODAY:

| 1 | 2 | 3 | 4 | 5 | 6 | 7 | 8 | 9 | 10 |

DISCONNECTED   CONNECTED

MEANINGFUL COINCIDENCES, THEMES, OR PATTERNS I ENCOUNTERED TODAY:

_____

_____

_____

INTUITIVE INSIGHTS I EXPERIENCED INTERNALLY OR PHYSICALLY:

_____

_____

THINGS THAT CONNECTED ME TO MY INTUITION TODAY:

☐ GETTING QUALITY QUIET TIME OR TIME ALONE

☐ MINDFULLY SLOWING DOWN

☐ LOWERING MY STRESS LEVELS

☐ HAVING NOURISHING WORK AND HOME ROUTINES

☐ KEEPING MY ENVIRONMENT TIDY AND INVITING

☐ LISTENING TO SOFT MUSIC OR NATURE SOUNDS

☐ PULLING AN ORACLE CARD FOR INSPIRATION

☐ OTHER:_____

WHERE/WHEN DID I FEEL MOST INTUITIVE TODAY?

_____

_____

WHAT WAS MOST ENCOURAGING, COMFORTING, OR EXCITING ABOUT
CONNECTING WITH MY INTUITION TODAY?

_____

_____

MORNING REFLECTION

DATE ___ / ___ / ___

HOW I'D RATE MY OPENNESS TO INTUITIVE GUIDANCE TODAY:

1   2   3   4   5   6   7   8   9   10

CLOSED/DISTRACTED   OPEN/GROUNDED

LAST NIGHT'S INTUITIVE DREAMS, OR INTUITIVE INSIGHTS WHEN I AWOKE:
_____
_____

TODAY I'D LIKE TO RECEIVE AN INTUITIVE SIGN ABOUT:
_____
_____

GOALS TO HELP ME FEEL LESS SCATTERED AND MORE CENTERED TODAY:
_____   _____
_____   _____

HOW I PLAN TO CONNECT MINDFULLY WITH MY INTUITION TODAY:
_____
_____
_____

MY MORNING INTUITIVE ROUTINE INCLUDED:

☐ MEDITATION   ☐ TIME IN NATURE   ☐ SELF-CARE:_____
☐ PRAYER   ☐ A HEALTHY BREAKFAST   ☐ OTHER:_____
☐ JOURNALING   ☐ SACRED PAUSES   _____

GUT CHECK—WHAT IS THE STRONGEST INSTINCT I HAVE RIGHT NOW ABOUT
HOW TO APPROACH A SITUATION, PERSON, OR ISSUE I'M FACING TODAY?
_____
_____
_____

EVENING REFLECTION

HOW I'D RATE MY ABILITY TO CONNECT WITH MY INTUITION TODAY:

1   2   3   4   5   6   7   8   9   10
DISCONNECTED   CONNECTED

MEANINGFUL COINCIDENCES, THEMES, OR PATTERNS I ENCOUNTERED TODAY:

_____

_____

_____

INTUITIVE INSIGHTS I EXPERIENCED INTERNALLY OR PHYSICALLY:

_____

_____

THINGS THAT CONNECTED ME TO MY INTUITION TODAY:

☐ GETTING QUALITY QUIET TIME OR TIME ALONE

☐ MINDFULLY SLOWING DOWN

☐ LOWERING MY STRESS LEVELS

☐ HAVING NOURISHING WORK AND HOME ROUTINES

☐ KEEPING MY ENVIRONMENT TIDY AND INVITING

☐ LISTENING TO SOFT MUSIC OR NATURE SOUNDS

☐ PULLING AN ORACLE CARD FOR INSPIRATION

☐ OTHER:_____

WHERE/WHEN DID I FEEL MOST INTUITIVE TODAY?

_____

_____

WHAT WAS MOST ENCOURAGING, COMFORTING, OR EXCITING ABOUT
CONNECTING WITH MY INTUITION TODAY?

_____

_____

MORNING REFLECTION   DATE ___/___/___

HOW I'D RATE MY OPENNESS TO INTUITIVE GUIDANCE TODAY:

1   2   3   4   5   6   7   8   9   10

CLOSED/DISTRACTED   OPEN/GROUNDED

LAST NIGHT'S INTUITIVE DREAMS, OR INTUITIVE INSIGHTS WHEN I AWOKE:

_____

_____

TODAY I'D LIKE TO RECEIVE AN INTUITIVE SIGN ABOUT:

_____

_____

GOALS TO HELP ME FEEL LESS SCATTERED AND MORE CENTERED TODAY:

_____   _____

_____   _____

HOW I PLAN TO CONNECT MINDFULLY WITH MY INTUITION TODAY:

_____

_____

_____

MY MORNING INTUITIVE ROUTINE INCLUDED:

☐ MEDITATION   ☐ TIME IN NATURE   ☐ SELF-CARE:_____

☐ PRAYER   ☐ A HEALTHY BREAKFAST   ☐ OTHER:_____

☐ JOURNALING   ☐ SACRED PAUSES   _____

GUT CHECK—WHAT IS THE STRONGEST INSTINCT I HAVE RIGHT NOW ABOUT
HOW TO APPROACH A SITUATION, PERSON, OR ISSUE I'M FACING TODAY?

_____

_____

_____

EVENING REFLECTION

HOW I'D RATE MY ABILITY TO CONNECT WITH MY INTUITION TODAY:

1	2	3	4	5	6	7	8	9	10

DISCONNECTED   CONNECTED

MEANINGFUL COINCIDENCES, THEMES, OR PATTERNS I ENCOUNTERED TODAY:

_____

_____

_____

INTUITIVE INSIGHTS I EXPERIENCED INTERNALLY OR PHYSICALLY:

_____

_____

THINGS THAT CONNECTED ME TO MY INTUITION TODAY:

- [ ] GETTING QUALITY QUIET TIME OR TIME ALONE
- [ ] MINDFULLY SLOWING DOWN
- [ ] LOWERING MY STRESS LEVELS
- [ ] HAVING NOURISHING WORK AND HOME ROUTINES
- [ ] KEEPING MY ENVIRONMENT TIDY AND INVITING
- [ ] LISTENING TO SOFT MUSIC OR NATURE SOUNDS
- [ ] PULLING AN ORACLE CARD FOR INSPIRATION
- [ ] OTHER:_____

WHERE/WHEN DID I FEEL MOST INTUITIVE TODAY?

_____

_____

WHAT WAS MOST ENCOURAGING, COMFORTING, OR EXCITING ABOUT
CONNECTING WITH MY INTUITION TODAY?

_____

_____

MORNING REFLECTION DATE ___/___/___

HOW I'D RATE MY OPENNESS TO INTUITIVE GUIDANCE TODAY:

1   2   3   4   5   6   7   8   9   10

CLOSED/DISTRACTED   OPEN/GROUNDED

LAST NIGHT'S INTUITIVE DREAMS, OR INTUITIVE INSIGHTS WHEN I AWOKE:

_____

_____

TODAY I'D LIKE TO RECEIVE AN INTUITIVE SIGN ABOUT:

_____

_____

GOALS TO HELP ME FEEL LESS SCATTERED AND MORE CENTERED TODAY:

_____   _____

_____   _____

HOW I PLAN TO CONNECT MINDFULLY WITH MY INTUITION TODAY:

_____

_____

_____

MY MORNING INTUITIVE ROUTINE INCLUDED:

☐ MEDITATION   ☐ TIME IN NATURE   ☐ SELF-CARE:_____

☐ PRAYER   ☐ A HEALTHY BREAKFAST   ☐ OTHER:_____

☐ JOURNALING   ☐ SACRED PAUSES   _____

GUT CHECK—WHAT IS THE STRONGEST INSTINCT I HAVE RIGHT NOW ABOUT
HOW TO APPROACH A SITUATION, PERSON, OR ISSUE I'M FACING TODAY?

_____

_____

_____

EVENING REFLECTION

HOW I'D RATE MY ABILITY TO CONNECT WITH MY INTUITION TODAY:

1   2   3   4   5   6   7   8   9   10

DISCONNECTED   CONNECTED

MEANINGFUL COINCIDENCES, THEMES, OR PATTERNS I ENCOUNTERED TODAY:

_____

_____

_____

INTUITIVE INSIGHTS I EXPERIENCED INTERNALLY OR PHYSICALLY:

_____

_____

THINGS THAT CONNECTED ME TO MY INTUITION TODAY:

☐ GETTING QUALITY QUIET TIME OR TIME ALONE

☐ MINDFULLY SLOWING DOWN

☐ LOWERING MY STRESS LEVELS

☐ HAVING NOURISHING WORK AND HOME ROUTINES

☐ KEEPING MY ENVIRONMENT TIDY AND INVITING

☐ LISTENING TO SOFT MUSIC OR NATURE SOUNDS

☐ PULLING AN ORACLE CARD FOR INSPIRATION

☐ OTHER:_____

WHERE/WHEN DID I FEEL MOST INTUITIVE TODAY?

_____

_____

WHAT WAS MOST ENCOURAGING, COMFORTING, OR EXCITING ABOUT
CONNECTING WITH MY INTUITION TODAY?

_____

_____

MORNING REFLECTION   DATE ___/___/___

HOW I'D RATE MY OPENNESS TO INTUITIVE GUIDANCE TODAY:

1   2   3   4   5   6   7   8   9   10

CLOSED/DISTRACTED   OPEN/GROUNDED

LAST NIGHT'S INTUITIVE DREAMS, OR INTUITIVE INSIGHTS WHEN I AWOKE:
_____
_____

TODAY I'D LIKE TO RECEIVE AN INTUITIVE SIGN ABOUT:
_____
_____

GOALS TO HELP ME FEEL LESS SCATTERED AND MORE CENTERED TODAY:
_____   _____
_____   _____

HOW I PLAN TO CONNECT MINDFULLY WITH MY INTUITION TODAY:
_____
_____
_____

MY MORNING INTUITIVE ROUTINE INCLUDED:

☐ MEDITATION   ☐ TIME IN NATURE   ☐ SELF-CARE:_____

☐ PRAYER   ☐ A HEALTHY BREAKFAST   ☐ OTHER:_____

☐ JOURNALING   ☐ SACRED PAUSES   _____

GUT CHECK—WHAT IS THE STRONGEST INSTINCT I HAVE RIGHT NOW ABOUT
HOW TO APPROACH A SITUATION, PERSON, OR ISSUE I'M FACING TODAY?
_____
_____
_____

EVENING REFLECTION

HOW I'D RATE MY ABILITY TO CONNECT WITH MY INTUITION TODAY:

1   2   3   4   5   6   7   8   9   10

DISCONNECTED   CONNECTED

MEANINGFUL COINCIDENCES, THEMES, OR PATTERNS I ENCOUNTERED TODAY:

_____

_____

_____

INTUITIVE INSIGHTS I EXPERIENCED INTERNALLY OR PHYSICALLY:

_____

_____

THINGS THAT CONNECTED ME TO MY INTUITION TODAY:

☐ GETTING QUALITY QUIET TIME OR TIME ALONE

☐ MINDFULLY SLOWING DOWN

☐ LOWERING MY STRESS LEVELS

☐ HAVING NOURISHING WORK AND HOME ROUTINES

☐ KEEPING MY ENVIRONMENT TIDY AND INVITING

☐ LISTENING TO SOFT MUSIC OR NATURE SOUNDS

☐ PULLING AN ORACLE CARD FOR INSPIRATION

☐ OTHER:_____

WHERE/WHEN DID I FEEL MOST INTUITIVE TODAY?

_____

_____

WHAT WAS MOST ENCOURAGING, COMFORTING, OR EXCITING ABOUT
CONNECTING WITH MY INTUITION TODAY?

_____

_____

MORNING REFLECTION   DATE ___/___/___

HOW I'D RATE MY OPENNESS TO INTUITIVE GUIDANCE TODAY:

1   2   3   4   5   6   7   8   9   10

CLOSED/DISTRACTED   OPEN/GROUNDED

LAST NIGHT'S INTUITIVE DREAMS, OR INTUITIVE INSIGHTS WHEN I AWOKE:
_____
_____

TODAY I'D LIKE TO RECEIVE AN INTUITIVE SIGN ABOUT:
_____
_____

GOALS TO HELP ME FEEL LESS SCATTERED AND MORE CENTERED TODAY:
_____   _____
_____   _____

HOW I PLAN TO CONNECT MINDFULLY WITH MY INTUITION TODAY:
_____
_____
_____

MY MORNING INTUITIVE ROUTINE INCLUDED:

☐ MEDITATION   ☐ TIME IN NATURE   ☐ SELF-CARE:_____

☐ PRAYER   ☐ A HEALTHY BREAKFAST ☐ OTHER:_____

☐ JOURNALING   ☐ SACRED PAUSES   _____

GUT CHECK—WHAT IS THE STRONGEST INSTINCT I HAVE RIGHT NOW ABOUT
HOW TO APPROACH A SITUATION, PERSON, OR ISSUE I'M FACING TODAY?
_____
_____

EVENING REFLECTION

HOW I'D RATE MY ABILITY TO CONNECT WITH MY INTUITION TODAY:

1   2   3   4   5   6   7   8   9   10

DISCONNECTED   CONNECTED

MEANINGFUL COINCIDENCES, THEMES, OR PATTERNS I ENCOUNTERED TODAY:

_____

_____

_____

INTUITIVE INSIGHTS I EXPERIENCED INTERNALLY OR PHYSICALLY:

_____

_____

THINGS THAT CONNECTED ME TO MY INTUITION TODAY:

☐ GETTING QUALITY QUIET TIME OR TIME ALONE

☐ MINDFULLY SLOWING DOWN

☐ LOWERING MY STRESS LEVELS

☐ HAVING NOURISHING WORK AND HOME ROUTINES

☐ KEEPING MY ENVIRONMENT TIDY AND INVITING

☐ LISTENING TO SOFT MUSIC OR NATURE SOUNDS

☐ PULLING AN ORACLE CARD FOR INSPIRATION

☐ OTHER:_____

WHERE/WHEN DID I FEEL MOST INTUITIVE TODAY?

_____

_____

WHAT WAS MOST ENCOURAGING, COMFORTING, OR EXCITING ABOUT
CONNECTING WITH MY INTUITION TODAY?

_____

_____

MORNING REFLECTION   DATE ___/___/___

LAST NIGHT'S INTUITIVE DREAMS, OR INTUITIVE INSIGHTS WHEN I AWOKE:
_____
_____

TODAY I'D LIKE TO RECEIVE AN INTUITIVE SIGN ABOUT:
_____
_____

GOALS TO HELP ME FEEL LESS SCATTERED AND MORE CENTERED TODAY:
_____   _____
_____   _____

HOW I PLAN TO CONNECT MINDFULLY WITH MY INTUITION TODAY:
_____
_____
_____

MY MORNING INTUITIVE ROUTINE INCLUDED:

☐ MEDITATION   ☐ TIME IN NATURE   ☐ SELF-CARE:_____
☐ PRAYER   ☐ A HEALTHY BREAKFAST   ☐ OTHER:_____
☐ JOURNALING   ☐ SACRED PAUSES   _____

GUT CHECK—WHAT IS THE STRONGEST INSTINCT I HAVE RIGHT NOW ABOUT
HOW TO APPROACH A SITUATION, PERSON, OR ISSUE I'M FACING TODAY?
_____
_____
_____

EVENING REFLECTION

HOW I'D RATE MY ABILITY TO CONNECT WITH MY INTUITION TODAY:

1   2   3   4   5   6   7   8   9   10

DISCONNECTED   CONNECTED

MEANINGFUL COINCIDENCES, THEMES, OR PATTERNS I ENCOUNTERED TODAY:

_____

_____

_____

INTUITIVE INSIGHTS I EXPERIENCED INTERNALLY OR PHYSICALLY:

_____

_____

THINGS THAT CONNECTED ME TO MY INTUITION TODAY:

☐ GETTING QUALITY QUIET TIME OR TIME ALONE

☐ MINDFULLY SLOWING DOWN

☐ LOWERING MY STRESS LEVELS

☐ HAVING NOURISHING WORK AND HOME ROUTINES

☐ KEEPING MY ENVIRONMENT TIDY AND INVITING

☐ LISTENING TO SOFT MUSIC OR NATURE SOUNDS

☐ PULLING AN ORACLE CARD FOR INSPIRATION

☐ OTHER:_____

WHERE/WHEN DID I FEEL MOST INTUITIVE TODAY?

_____

_____

WHAT WAS MOST ENCOURAGING, COMFORTING, OR EXCITING ABOUT
CONNECTING WITH MY INTUITION TODAY?

_____

_____

MORNING REFLECTION

DATE ___/___/___

HOW I'D RATE MY OPENNESS TO INTUITIVE GUIDANCE TODAY:

1   2   3   4   5   6   7   8   9   10

CLOSED/DISTRACTED   OPEN/GROUNDED

LAST NIGHT'S INTUITIVE DREAMS, OR INTUITIVE INSIGHTS WHEN I AWOKE:
_____
_____

TODAY I'D LIKE TO RECEIVE AN INTUITIVE SIGN ABOUT:
_____
_____

GOALS TO HELP ME FEEL LESS SCATTERED AND MORE CENTERED TODAY:
_____   _____
_____   _____

HOW I PLAN TO CONNECT MINDFULLY WITH MY INTUITION TODAY:
_____
_____
_____

MY MORNING INTUITIVE ROUTINE INCLUDED:

☐ MEDITATION   ☐ TIME IN NATURE   ☐ SELF-CARE:_____
☐ PRAYER   ☐ A HEALTHY BREAKFAST   ☐ OTHER:_____
☐ JOURNALING   ☐ SACRED PAUSES   _____

GUT CHECK—WHAT IS THE STRONGEST INSTINCT I HAVE RIGHT NOW ABOUT
HOW TO APPROACH A SITUATION, PERSON, OR ISSUE I'M FACING TODAY?
_____
_____
_____

EVENING REFLECTION

HOW I'D RATE MY ABILITY TO CONNECT WITH MY INTUITION TODAY:

1   2   3   4   5   6   7   8   9   10

DISCONNECTED   CONNECTED

MEANINGFUL COINCIDENCES, THEMES, OR PATTERNS I ENCOUNTERED TODAY:

_____

_____

_____

INTUITIVE INSIGHTS I EXPERIENCED INTERNALLY OR PHYSICALLY:

_____

_____

THINGS THAT CONNECTED ME TO MY INTUITION TODAY:

☐ GETTING QUALITY QUIET TIME OR TIME ALONE

☐ MINDFULLY SLOWING DOWN

☐ LOWERING MY STRESS LEVELS

☐ HAVING NOURISHING WORK AND HOME ROUTINES

☐ KEEPING MY ENVIRONMENT TIDY AND INVITING

☐ LISTENING TO SOFT MUSIC OR NATURE SOUNDS

☐ PULLING AN ORACLE CARD FOR INSPIRATION

☐ OTHER:_____

WHERE/WHEN DID I FEEL MOST INTUITIVE TODAY?

_____

_____

WHAT WAS MOST ENCOURAGING, COMFORTING, OR EXCITING ABOUT
CONNECTING WITH MY INTUITION TODAY?

_____

_____

MORNING REFLECTION

DATE ___/___/___

HOW I'D RATE MY OPENNESS TO INTUITIVE GUIDANCE TODAY:

1   2   3   4   5   6   7   8   9   10

CLOSED/DISTRACTED   OPEN/GROUNDED

LAST NIGHT'S INTUITIVE DREAMS, OR INTUITIVE INSIGHTS WHEN I AWOKE:

_____

_____

TODAY I'D LIKE TO RECEIVE AN INTUITIVE SIGN ABOUT:

_____

_____

GOALS TO HELP ME FEEL LESS SCATTERED AND MORE CENTERED TODAY:

_____   _____

_____   _____

HOW I PLAN TO CONNECT MINDFULLY WITH MY INTUITION TODAY:

_____

_____

_____

MY MORNING INTUITIVE ROUTINE INCLUDED:

☐ MEDITATION   ☐ TIME IN NATURE   ☐ SELF-CARE:_____

☐ PRAYER   ☐ A HEALTHY BREAKFAST   ☐ OTHER:_____

☐ JOURNALING   ☐ SACRED PAUSES   _____

GUT CHECK—WHAT IS THE STRONGEST INSTINCT I HAVE RIGHT NOW ABOUT
HOW TO APPROACH A SITUATION, PERSON, OR ISSUE I'M FACING TODAY?

_____

_____

_____

EVENING REFLECTION

HOW I'D RATE MY ABILITY TO CONNECT WITH MY INTUITION TODAY:

1	2	3	4	5	6	7	8	9	10

DISCONNECTED   CONNECTED

MEANINGFUL COINCIDENCES, THEMES, OR PATTERNS I ENCOUNTERED TODAY:
_____
_____
_____

INTUITIVE INSIGHTS I EXPERIENCED INTERNALLY OR PHYSICALLY:
_____
_____

THINGS THAT CONNECTED ME TO MY INTUITION TODAY:

☐ GETTING QUALITY QUIET TIME OR TIME ALONE

☐ MINDFULLY SLOWING DOWN

☐ LOWERING MY STRESS LEVELS

☐ HAVING NOURISHING WORK AND HOME ROUTINES

☐ KEEPING MY ENVIRONMENT TIDY AND INVITING

☐ LISTENING TO SOFT MUSIC OR NATURE SOUNDS

☐ PULLING AN ORACLE CARD FOR INSPIRATION

☐ OTHER:_____

WHERE/WHEN DID I FEEL MOST INTUITIVE TODAY?
_____
_____

WHAT WAS MOST ENCOURAGING, COMFORTING, OR EXCITING ABOUT
CONNECTING WITH MY INTUITION TODAY?
_____
_____

MORNING REFLECTION

DATE ___/___/___

HOW I'D RATE MY OPENNESS TO INTUITIVE GUIDANCE TODAY:

1   2   3   4   5   6   7   8   9   10

CLOSED/DISTRACTED   OPEN/GROUNDED

LAST NIGHT'S INTUITIVE DREAMS, OR INTUITIVE INSIGHTS WHEN I AWOKE:

_____

_____

TODAY I'D LIKE TO RECEIVE AN INTUITIVE SIGN ABOUT:

_____

_____

GOALS TO HELP ME FEEL LESS SCATTERED AND MORE CENTERED TODAY:

_____   _____

_____   _____

HOW I PLAN TO CONNECT MINDFULLY WITH MY INTUITION TODAY:

_____

_____

_____

MY MORNING INTUITIVE ROUTINE INCLUDED:

☐ MEDITATION   ☐ TIME IN NATURE   ☐ SELF-CARE:_____

☐ PRAYER   ☐ A HEALTHY BREAKFAST   ☐ OTHER:_____

☐ JOURNALING   ☐ SACRED PAUSES   _____

GUT CHECK—WHAT IS THE STRONGEST INSTINCT I HAVE RIGHT NOW ABOUT
HOW TO APPROACH A SITUATION, PERSON, OR ISSUE I'M FACING TODAY?

_____

_____

_____

EVENING REFLECTION

HOW I'D RATE MY ABILITY TO CONNECT WITH MY INTUITION TODAY:

1   2   3   4   5   6   7   8   9   10

DISCONNECTED   CONNECTED

MEANINGFUL COINCIDENCES, THEMES, OR PATTERNS I ENCOUNTERED TODAY:

_____

_____

_____

INTUITIVE INSIGHTS I EXPERIENCED INTERNALLY OR PHYSICALLY:

_____

_____

THINGS THAT CONNECTED ME TO MY INTUITION TODAY:

☐ GETTING QUALITY QUIET TIME OR TIME ALONE

☐ MINDFULLY SLOWING DOWN

☐ LOWERING MY STRESS LEVELS

☐ HAVING NOURISHING WORK AND HOME ROUTINES

☐ KEEPING MY ENVIRONMENT TIDY AND INVITING

☐ LISTENING TO SOFT MUSIC OR NATURE SOUNDS

☐ PULLING AN ORACLE CARD FOR INSPIRATION

☐ OTHER:_____

WHERE/WHEN DID I FEEL MOST INTUITIVE TODAY?

_____

_____

WHAT WAS MOST ENCOURAGING, COMFORTING, OR EXCITING ABOUT
CONNECTING WITH MY INTUITION TODAY?

_____

_____

MORNING REFLECTION

DATE ___/___/___

HOW I'D RATE MY OPENNESS TO INTUITIVE GUIDANCE TODAY:

1   2   3   4   5   6   7   8   9   10

CLOSED/DISTRACTED   OPEN/GROUNDED

LAST NIGHT'S INTUITIVE DREAMS, OR INTUITIVE INSIGHTS WHEN I AWOKE:

_____

_____

TODAY I'D LIKE TO RECEIVE AN INTUITIVE SIGN ABOUT:

_____

_____

GOALS TO HELP ME FEEL LESS SCATTERED AND MORE CENTERED TODAY:

_____   _____

_____   _____

HOW I PLAN TO CONNECT MINDFULLY WITH MY INTUITION TODAY:

_____

_____

_____

MY MORNING INTUITIVE ROUTINE INCLUDED:

☐ MEDITATION   ☐ TIME IN NATURE   ☐ SELF-CARE:_____
☐ PRAYER   ☐ A HEALTHY BREAKFAST   ☐ OTHER:_____
☐ JOURNALING   ☐ SACRED PAUSES   _____

GUT CHECK—WHAT IS THE STRONGEST INSTINCT I HAVE RIGHT NOW ABOUT
HOW TO APPROACH A SITUATION, PERSON, OR ISSUE I'M FACING TODAY?

_____

_____

_____

EVENING REFLECTION

HOW I'D RATE MY ABILITY TO CONNECT WITH MY INTUITION TODAY:

1	2	3	4	5	6	7	8	9	10

DISCONNECTED   CONNECTED

MEANINGFUL COINCIDENCES, THEMES, OR PATTERNS I ENCOUNTERED TODAY:

_____

_____

_____

INTUITIVE INSIGHTS I EXPERIENCED INTERNALLY OR PHYSICALLY:

_____

_____

THINGS THAT CONNECTED ME TO MY INTUITION TODAY:

- [ ] GETTING QUALITY QUIET TIME OR TIME ALONE
- [ ] MINDFULLY SLOWING DOWN
- [ ] LOWERING MY STRESS LEVELS
- [ ] HAVING NOURISHING WORK AND HOME ROUTINES
- [ ] KEEPING MY ENVIRONMENT TIDY AND INVITING
- [ ] LISTENING TO SOFT MUSIC OR NATURE SOUNDS
- [ ] PULLING AN ORACLE CARD FOR INSPIRATION
- [ ] OTHER:_____

WHERE/WHEN DID I FEEL MOST INTUITIVE TODAY?

_____

_____

WHAT WAS MOST ENCOURAGING, COMFORTING, OR EXCITING ABOUT
CONNECTING WITH MY INTUITION TODAY?

_____

_____

MORNING REFLECTION

DATE ___ / ___ / ___

HOW I'D RATE MY OPENNESS TO INTUITIVE GUIDANCE TODAY:

1   2   3   4   5   6   7   8   9   10

CLOSED/DISTRACTED   OPEN/GROUNDED

LAST NIGHT'S INTUITIVE DREAMS, OR INTUITIVE INSIGHTS WHEN I AWOKE:

_____

_____

TODAY I'D LIKE TO RECEIVE AN INTUITIVE SIGN ABOUT:

_____

_____

GOALS TO HELP ME FEEL LESS SCATTERED AND MORE CENTERED TODAY:

_____   _____

_____   _____

HOW I PLAN TO CONNECT MINDFULLY WITH MY INTUITION TODAY:

_____

_____

_____

MY MORNING INTUITIVE ROUTINE INCLUDED:

☐ MEDITATION   ☐ TIME IN NATURE   ☐ SELF-CARE:_____

☐ PRAYER   ☐ A HEALTHY BREAKFAST   ☐ OTHER:_____

☐ JOURNALING   ☐ SACRED PAUSES   _____

GUT CHECK—WHAT IS THE STRONGEST INSTINCT I HAVE RIGHT NOW ABOUT
HOW TO APPROACH A SITUATION, PERSON, OR ISSUE I'M FACING TODAY?

_____

_____

EVENING REFLECTION

HOW I'D RATE MY ABILITY TO CONNECT WITH MY INTUITION TODAY:

1	2	3	4	5	6	7	8	9	10

DISCONNECTED   CONNECTED

MEANINGFUL COINCIDENCES, THEMES, OR PATTERNS I ENCOUNTERED TODAY:
_____
_____
_____

INTUITIVE INSIGHTS I EXPERIENCED INTERNALLY OR PHYSICALLY:
_____
_____

THINGS THAT CONNECTED ME TO MY INTUITION TODAY:

- ☐ GETTING QUALITY QUIET TIME OR TIME ALONE
- ☐ MINDFULLY SLOWING DOWN
- ☐ LOWERING MY STRESS LEVELS
- ☐ HAVING NOURISHING WORK AND HOME ROUTINES
- ☐ KEEPING MY ENVIRONMENT TIDY AND INVITING
- ☐ LISTENING TO SOFT MUSIC OR NATURE SOUNDS
- ☐ PULLING AN ORACLE CARD FOR INSPIRATION
- ☐ OTHER:_____

WHERE/WHEN DID I FEEL MOST INTUITIVE TODAY?
_____
_____

WHAT WAS MOST ENCOURAGING, COMFORTING, OR EXCITING ABOUT
CONNECTING WITH MY INTUITION TODAY?
_____
_____

MORNING REFLECTION DATE ___/___/___

HOW I'D RATE MY OPENNESS TO INTUITIVE GUIDANCE TODAY:

1   2   3   4   5   6   7   8   9   10

CLOSED/DISTRACTED   OPEN/GROUNDED

LAST NIGHT'S INTUITIVE DREAMS, OR INTUITIVE INSIGHTS WHEN I AWOKE:

_____

_____

TODAY I'D LIKE TO RECEIVE AN INTUITIVE SIGN ABOUT:

_____

_____

GOALS TO HELP ME FEEL LESS SCATTERED AND MORE CENTERED TODAY:

_____   _____

_____   _____

HOW I PLAN TO CONNECT MINDFULLY WITH MY INTUITION TODAY:

_____

_____

_____

MY MORNING INTUITIVE ROUTINE INCLUDED:

☐ MEDITATION   ☐ TIME IN NATURE   ☐ SELF-CARE:_____

☐ PRAYER   ☐ A HEALTHY BREAKFAST ☐ OTHER:_____

☐ JOURNALING   ☐ SACRED PAUSES   _____

GUT CHECK—WHAT IS THE STRONGEST INSTINCT I HAVE RIGHT NOW ABOUT
HOW TO APPROACH A SITUATION, PERSON, OR ISSUE I'M FACING TODAY?

_____

_____

_____

EVENING REFLECTION

HOW I'D RATE MY ABILITY TO CONNECT WITH MY INTUITION TODAY:

1   2   3   4   5   6   7   8   9   10

DISCONNECTED   CONNECTED

MEANINGFUL COINCIDENCES, THEMES, OR PATTERNS I ENCOUNTERED TODAY:

_____

_____

_____

INTUITIVE INSIGHTS I EXPERIENCED INTERNALLY OR PHYSICALLY:

_____

_____

THINGS THAT CONNECTED ME TO MY INTUITION TODAY:

- [ ] GETTING QUALITY QUIET TIME OR TIME ALONE
- [ ] MINDFULLY SLOWING DOWN
- [ ] LOWERING MY STRESS LEVELS
- [ ] HAVING NOURISHING WORK AND HOME ROUTINES
- [ ] KEEPING MY ENVIRONMENT TIDY AND INVITING
- [ ] LISTENING TO SOFT MUSIC OR NATURE SOUNDS
- [ ] PULLING AN ORACLE CARD FOR INSPIRATION
- [ ] OTHER:_____

WHERE/WHEN DID I FEEL MOST INTUITIVE TODAY?

_____

_____

WHAT WAS MOST ENCOURAGING, COMFORTING, OR EXCITING ABOUT
CONNECTING WITH MY INTUITION TODAY?

_____

_____

MORNING REFLECTION

DATE ___/___/___

HOW I'D RATE MY OPENNESS TO INTUITIVE GUIDANCE TODAY:

1   2   3   4   5   6   7   8   9   10

CLOSED/DISTRACTED   OPEN/GROUNDED

LAST NIGHT'S INTUITIVE DREAMS, OR INTUITIVE INSIGHTS WHEN I AWOKE:

_____

_____

TODAY I'D LIKE TO RECEIVE AN INTUITIVE SIGN ABOUT:

_____

_____

GOALS TO HELP ME FEEL LESS SCATTERED AND MORE CENTERED TODAY:

_____   _____

_____   _____

HOW I PLAN TO CONNECT MINDFULLY WITH MY INTUITION TODAY:

_____

_____

_____

MY MORNING INTUITIVE ROUTINE INCLUDED:

☐ MEDITATION   ☐ TIME IN NATURE   ☐ SELF-CARE:_____

☐ PRAYER   ☐ A HEALTHY BREAKFAST   ☐ OTHER:_____

☐ JOURNALING   ☐ SACRED PAUSES   _____

GUT CHECK—WHAT IS THE STRONGEST INSTINCT I HAVE RIGHT NOW ABOUT
HOW TO APPROACH A SITUATION, PERSON, OR ISSUE I'M FACING TODAY?

_____

_____

_____

EVENING REFLECTION

HOW I'D RATE MY ABILITY TO CONNECT WITH MY INTUITION TODAY:

1   2   3   4   5   6   7   8   9   10

DISCONNECTED   CONNECTED

MEANINGFUL COINCIDENCES, THEMES, OR PATTERNS I ENCOUNTERED TODAY:

_____

_____

_____

INTUITIVE INSIGHTS I EXPERIENCED INTERNALLY OR PHYSICALLY:

_____

_____

THINGS THAT CONNECTED ME TO MY INTUITION TODAY:

☐ GETTING QUALITY QUIET TIME OR TIME ALONE

☐ MINDFULLY SLOWING DOWN

☐ LOWERING MY STRESS LEVELS

☐ HAVING NOURISHING WORK AND HOME ROUTINES

☐ KEEPING MY ENVIRONMENT TIDY AND INVITING

☐ LISTENING TO SOFT MUSIC OR NATURE SOUNDS

☐ PULLING AN ORACLE CARD FOR INSPIRATION

☐ OTHER:_____

WHERE/WHEN DID I FEEL MOST INTUITIVE TODAY?

_____

_____

WHAT WAS MOST ENCOURAGING, COMFORTING, OR EXCITING ABOUT
CONNECTING WITH MY INTUITION TODAY?

_____

_____

MORNING REFLECTION   DATE ___/___/___

LAST NIGHT'S INTUITIVE DREAMS, OR INTUITIVE INSIGHTS WHEN I AWOKE:
_____
_____

TODAY I'D LIKE TO RECEIVE AN INTUITIVE SIGN ABOUT:
_____
_____

GOALS TO HELP ME FEEL LESS SCATTERED AND MORE CENTERED TODAY:
_____   _____
_____   _____

HOW I PLAN TO CONNECT MINDFULLY WITH MY INTUITION TODAY:
_____
_____
_____

MY MORNING INTUITIVE ROUTINE INCLUDED:

☐ MEDITATION   ☐ TIME IN NATURE   ☐ SELF-CARE:_____
☐ PRAYER   ☐ A HEALTHY BREAKFAST   ☐ OTHER:_____
☐ JOURNALING   ☐ SACRED PAUSES   _____

GUT CHECK—WHAT IS THE STRONGEST INSTINCT I HAVE RIGHT NOW ABOUT
HOW TO APPROACH A SITUATION, PERSON, OR ISSUE I'M FACING TODAY?
_____
_____
_____

EVENING REFLECTION

HOW I'D RATE MY ABILITY TO CONNECT WITH MY INTUITION TODAY:

1   2   3   4   5   6   7   8   9   10

DISCONNECTED   CONNECTED

MEANINGFUL COINCIDENCES, THEMES, OR PATTERNS I ENCOUNTERED TODAY:
_____
_____
_____

INTUITIVE INSIGHTS I EXPERIENCED INTERNALLY OR PHYSICALLY:
_____
_____

THINGS THAT CONNECTED ME TO MY INTUITION TODAY:

☐ GETTING QUALITY QUIET TIME OR TIME ALONE

☐ MINDFULLY SLOWING DOWN

☐ LOWERING MY STRESS LEVELS

☐ HAVING NOURISHING WORK AND HOME ROUTINES

☐ KEEPING MY ENVIRONMENT TIDY AND INVITING

☐ LISTENING TO SOFT MUSIC OR NATURE SOUNDS

☐ PULLING AN ORACLE CARD FOR INSPIRATION

☐ OTHER:_____

WHERE/WHEN DID I FEEL MOST INTUITIVE TODAY?
_____
_____

WHAT WAS MOST ENCOURAGING, COMFORTING, OR EXCITING ABOUT
CONNECTING WITH MY INTUITION TODAY?
_____
_____

MORNING REFLECTION DATE ___ / ___ / ___

HOW I'D RATE MY OPENNESS TO INTUITIVE GUIDANCE TODAY:

1   2   3   4   5   6   7   8   9   10

CLOSED/DISTRACTED   OPEN/GROUNDED

LAST NIGHT'S INTUITIVE DREAMS, OR INTUITIVE INSIGHTS WHEN I AWOKE:

_____

_____

TODAY I'D LIKE TO RECEIVE AN INTUITIVE SIGN ABOUT:

_____

_____

GOALS TO HELP ME FEEL LESS SCATTERED AND MORE CENTERED TODAY:

_____   _____

_____   _____

HOW I PLAN TO CONNECT MINDFULLY WITH MY INTUITION TODAY:

_____

_____

_____

MY MORNING INTUITIVE ROUTINE INCLUDED:

☐ MEDITATION   ☐ TIME IN NATURE   ☐ SELF-CARE:_____

☐ PRAYER   ☐ A HEALTHY BREAKFAST   ☐ OTHER:_____

☐ JOURNALING   ☐ SACRED PAUSES   _____

GUT CHECK—WHAT IS THE STRONGEST INSTINCT I HAVE RIGHT NOW ABOUT
HOW TO APPROACH A SITUATION, PERSON, OR ISSUE I'M FACING TODAY?

_____

_____

_____

EVENING REFLECTION

HOW I'D RATE MY ABILITY TO CONNECT WITH MY INTUITION TODAY:

1   2   3   4   5   6   7   8   9   10

DISCONNECTED   CONNECTED

MEANINGFUL COINCIDENCES, THEMES, OR PATTERNS I ENCOUNTERED TODAY:

_____

_____

_____

INTUITIVE INSIGHTS I EXPERIENCED INTERNALLY OR PHYSICALLY:

_____

_____

THINGS THAT CONNECTED ME TO MY INTUITION TODAY:

- [ ] GETTING QUALITY QUIET TIME OR TIME ALONE
- [ ] MINDFULLY SLOWING DOWN
- [ ] LOWERING MY STRESS LEVELS
- [ ] HAVING NOURISHING WORK AND HOME ROUTINES
- [ ] KEEPING MY ENVIRONMENT TIDY AND INVITING
- [ ] LISTENING TO SOFT MUSIC OR NATURE SOUNDS
- [ ] PULLING AN ORACLE CARD FOR INSPIRATION
- [ ] OTHER:_____

WHERE/WHEN DID I FEEL MOST INTUITIVE TODAY?

_____

_____

WHAT WAS MOST ENCOURAGING, COMFORTING, OR EXCITING ABOUT
CONNECTING WITH MY INTUITION TODAY?

_____

_____

MORNING REFLECTION

DATE ___/___/___

HOW I'D RATE MY OPENNESS TO INTUITIVE GUIDANCE TODAY:

1   2   3   4   5   6   7   8   9   10

CLOSED/DISTRACTED   OPEN/GROUNDED

LAST NIGHT'S INTUITIVE DREAMS, OR INTUITIVE INSIGHTS WHEN I AWOKE:

_____

_____

TODAY I'D LIKE TO RECEIVE AN INTUITIVE SIGN ABOUT:

_____

_____

GOALS TO HELP ME FEEL LESS SCATTERED AND MORE CENTERED TODAY:

_____   _____

_____   _____

HOW I PLAN TO CONNECT MINDFULLY WITH MY INTUITION TODAY:

_____

_____

_____

MY MORNING INTUITIVE ROUTINE INCLUDED:

☐ MEDITATION   ☐ TIME IN NATURE   ☐ SELF-CARE:_____

☐ PRAYER   ☐ A HEALTHY BREAKFAST   ☐ OTHER:_____

☐ JOURNALING   ☐ SACRED PAUSES   _____

GUT CHECK—WHAT IS THE STRONGEST INSTINCT I HAVE RIGHT NOW ABOUT
HOW TO APPROACH A SITUATION, PERSON, OR ISSUE I'M FACING TODAY?

_____

_____

_____

EVENING REFLECTION

HOW I'D RATE MY ABILITY TO CONNECT WITH MY INTUITION TODAY:

1   2   3   4   5   6   7   8   9   10

DISCONNECTED   CONNECTED

MEANINGFUL COINCIDENCES, THEMES, OR PATTERNS I ENCOUNTERED TODAY:
_____
_____
_____

INTUITIVE INSIGHTS I EXPERIENCED INTERNALLY OR PHYSICALLY:
_____
_____

THINGS THAT CONNECTED ME TO MY INTUITION TODAY:

☐ GETTING QUALITY QUIET TIME OR TIME ALONE

☐ MINDFULLY SLOWING DOWN

☐ LOWERING MY STRESS LEVELS

☐ HAVING NOURISHING WORK AND HOME ROUTINES

☐ KEEPING MY ENVIRONMENT TIDY AND INVITING

☐ LISTENING TO SOFT MUSIC OR NATURE SOUNDS

☐ PULLING AN ORACLE CARD FOR INSPIRATION

☐ OTHER:_____

WHERE/WHEN DID I FEEL MOST INTUITIVE TODAY?
_____
_____

WHAT WAS MOST ENCOURAGING, COMFORTING, OR EXCITING ABOUT
CONNECTING WITH MY INTUITION TODAY?
_____
_____

MORNING REFLECTION

DATE ___/___/___

HOW I'D RATE MY OPENNESS TO INTUITIVE GUIDANCE TODAY:

1   2   3   4   5   6   7   8   9   10

CLOSED/DISTRACTED   OPEN/GROUNDED

LAST NIGHT'S INTUITIVE DREAMS, OR INTUITIVE INSIGHTS WHEN I AWOKE:

_____

_____

TODAY I'D LIKE TO RECEIVE AN INTUITIVE SIGN ABOUT:

_____

_____

GOALS TO HELP ME FEEL LESS SCATTERED AND MORE CENTERED TODAY:

_____   _____

_____   _____

HOW I PLAN TO CONNECT MINDFULLY WITH MY INTUITION TODAY:

_____

_____

_____

MY MORNING INTUITIVE ROUTINE INCLUDED:

☐ MEDITATION   ☐ TIME IN NATURE   ☐ SELF-CARE:_____

☐ PRAYER   ☐ A HEALTHY BREAKFAST   ☐ OTHER:_____

☐ JOURNALING   ☐ SACRED PAUSES   _____

GUT CHECK—WHAT IS THE STRONGEST INSTINCT I HAVE RIGHT NOW ABOUT
HOW TO APPROACH A SITUATION, PERSON, OR ISSUE I'M FACING TODAY?

_____

_____

_____

EVENING REFLECTION

HOW I'D RATE MY ABILITY TO CONNECT WITH MY INTUITION TODAY:

1	2	3	4	5	6	7	8	9	10

DISCONNECTED   CONNECTED

MEANINGFUL COINCIDENCES, THEMES, OR PATTERNS I ENCOUNTERED TODAY:
_____
_____
_____

INTUITIVE INSIGHTS I EXPERIENCED INTERNALLY OR PHYSICALLY:
_____
_____

THINGS THAT CONNECTED ME TO MY INTUITION TODAY:

☐ GETTING QUALITY QUIET TIME OR TIME ALONE

☐ MINDFULLY SLOWING DOWN

☐ LOWERING MY STRESS LEVELS

☐ HAVING NOURISHING WORK AND HOME ROUTINES

☐ KEEPING MY ENVIRONMENT TIDY AND INVITING

☐ LISTENING TO SOFT MUSIC OR NATURE SOUNDS

☐ PULLING AN ORACLE CARD FOR INSPIRATION

☐ OTHER:_____

WHERE/WHEN DID I FEEL MOST INTUITIVE TODAY?
_____
_____

WHAT WAS MOST ENCOURAGING, COMFORTING, OR EXCITING ABOUT
CONNECTING WITH MY INTUITION TODAY?
_____
_____

MORNING REFLECTION DATE ___/___/___

HOW I'D RATE MY OPENNESS TO INTUITIVE GUIDANCE TODAY:

1   2   3   4   5   6   7   8   9   10

CLOSED/DISTRACTED   OPEN/GROUNDED

LAST NIGHT'S INTUITIVE DREAMS, OR INTUITIVE INSIGHTS WHEN I AWOKE:
_____
_____

TODAY I'D LIKE TO RECEIVE AN INTUITIVE SIGN ABOUT:
_____
_____

GOALS TO HELP ME FEEL LESS SCATTERED AND MORE CENTERED TODAY:
_____   _____
_____   _____

HOW I PLAN TO CONNECT MINDFULLY WITH MY INTUITION TODAY:
_____
_____
_____

MY MORNING INTUITIVE ROUTINE INCLUDED:

☐ MEDITATION   ☐ TIME IN NATURE   ☐ SELF-CARE:_____

☐ PRAYER   ☐ A HEALTHY BREAKFAST   ☐ OTHER:_____

☐ JOURNALING   ☐ SACRED PAUSES   _____

GUT CHECK—WHAT IS THE STRONGEST INSTINCT I HAVE RIGHT NOW ABOUT
HOW TO APPROACH A SITUATION, PERSON, OR ISSUE I'M FACING TODAY?
_____
_____
_____

EVENING REFLECTION

HOW I'D RATE MY ABILITY TO CONNECT WITH MY INTUITION TODAY:

1   2   3   4   5   6   7   8   9   10

DISCONNECTED   CONNECTED

MEANINGFUL COINCIDENCES, THEMES, OR PATTERNS I ENCOUNTERED TODAY:

_____

_____

_____

INTUITIVE INSIGHTS I EXPERIENCED INTERNALLY OR PHYSICALLY:

_____

_____

THINGS THAT CONNECTED ME TO MY INTUITION TODAY:

- [ ] GETTING QUALITY QUIET TIME OR TIME ALONE
- [ ] MINDFULLY SLOWING DOWN
- [ ] LOWERING MY STRESS LEVELS
- [ ] HAVING NOURISHING WORK AND HOME ROUTINES
- [ ] KEEPING MY ENVIRONMENT TIDY AND INVITING
- [ ] LISTENING TO SOFT MUSIC OR NATURE SOUNDS
- [ ] PULLING AN ORACLE CARD FOR INSPIRATION
- [ ] OTHER:_____

WHERE/WHEN DID I FEEL MOST INTUITIVE TODAY?

_____

_____

WHAT WAS MOST ENCOURAGING, COMFORTING, OR EXCITING ABOUT
CONNECTING WITH MY INTUITION TODAY?

_____

_____

MORNING REFLECTION

DATE ___/___/___

HOW I'D RATE MY OPENNESS TO INTUITIVE GUIDANCE TODAY:

1   2   3   4   5   6   7   8   9   10

CLOSED/DISTRACTED   OPEN/GROUNDED

LAST NIGHT'S INTUITIVE DREAMS, OR INTUITIVE INSIGHTS WHEN I AWOKE:
_____
_____

TODAY I'D LIKE TO RECEIVE AN INTUITIVE SIGN ABOUT:
_____
_____

GOALS TO HELP ME FEEL LESS SCATTERED AND MORE CENTERED TODAY:
_____   _____
_____   _____

HOW I PLAN TO CONNECT MINDFULLY WITH MY INTUITION TODAY:
_____
_____
_____

MY MORNING INTUITIVE ROUTINE INCLUDED:

☐ MEDITATION   ☐ TIME IN NATURE   ☐ SELF-CARE:_____
☐ PRAYER   ☐ A HEALTHY BREAKFAST   ☐ OTHER:_____
☐ JOURNALING   ☐ SACRED PAUSES   _____

GUT CHECK—WHAT IS THE STRONGEST INSTINCT I HAVE RIGHT NOW ABOUT
HOW TO APPROACH A SITUATION, PERSON, OR ISSUE I'M FACING TODAY?
_____
_____
_____

EVENING REFLECTION

HOW I'D RATE MY ABILITY TO CONNECT WITH MY INTUITION TODAY:

1   2   3   4   5   6   7   8   9   10

DISCONNECTED   CONNECTED

MEANINGFUL COINCIDENCES, THEMES, OR PATTERNS I ENCOUNTERED TODAY:

_____

_____

_____

INTUITIVE INSIGHTS I EXPERIENCED INTERNALLY OR PHYSICALLY:

_____

_____

THINGS THAT CONNECTED ME TO MY INTUITION TODAY:

☐ GETTING QUALITY QUIET TIME OR TIME ALONE

☐ MINDFULLY SLOWING DOWN

☐ LOWERING MY STRESS LEVELS

☐ HAVING NOURISHING WORK AND HOME ROUTINES

☐ KEEPING MY ENVIRONMENT TIDY AND INVITING

☐ LISTENING TO SOFT MUSIC OR NATURE SOUNDS

☐ PULLING AN ORACLE CARD FOR INSPIRATION

☐ OTHER:_____

WHERE/WHEN DID I FEEL MOST INTUITIVE TODAY?

_____

_____

WHAT WAS MOST ENCOURAGING, COMFORTING, OR EXCITING ABOUT
CONNECTING WITH MY INTUITION TODAY?

_____

_____

MORNING REFLECTION   DATE ___/___/___

HOW I'D RATE MY OPENNESS TO INTUITIVE GUIDANCE TODAY:

1   2   3   4   5   6   7   8   9   10

CLOSED/DISTRACTED   OPEN/GROUNDED

LAST NIGHT'S INTUITIVE DREAMS, OR INTUITIVE INSIGHTS WHEN I AWOKE:

_____

_____

TODAY I'D LIKE TO RECEIVE AN INTUITIVE SIGN ABOUT:

_____

_____

GOALS TO HELP ME FEEL LESS SCATTERED AND MORE CENTERED TODAY:

_____   _____

_____   _____

HOW I PLAN TO CONNECT MINDFULLY WITH MY INTUITION TODAY:

_____

_____

_____

MY MORNING INTUITIVE ROUTINE INCLUDED:

☐ MEDITATION   ☐ TIME IN NATURE   ☐ SELF-CARE:_____

☐ PRAYER   ☐ A HEALTHY BREAKFAST   ☐ OTHER:_____

☐ JOURNALING   ☐ SACRED PAUSES   _____

GUT CHECK—WHAT IS THE STRONGEST INSTINCT I HAVE RIGHT NOW ABOUT
HOW TO APPROACH A SITUATION, PERSON, OR ISSUE I'M FACING TODAY?

_____

_____

EVENING REFLECTION

HOW I'D RATE MY ABILITY TO CONNECT WITH MY INTUITION TODAY:

1   2   3   4   5   6   7   8   9   10

DISCONNECTED   CONNECTED

MEANINGFUL COINCIDENCES, THEMES, OR PATTERNS I ENCOUNTERED TODAY:

_____

_____

_____

INTUITIVE INSIGHTS I EXPERIENCED INTERNALLY OR PHYSICALLY:

_____

_____

THINGS THAT CONNECTED ME TO MY INTUITION TODAY:

- [ ] GETTING QUALITY QUIET TIME OR TIME ALONE
- [ ] MINDFULLY SLOWING DOWN
- [ ] LOWERING MY STRESS LEVELS
- [ ] HAVING NOURISHING WORK AND HOME ROUTINES
- [ ] KEEPING MY ENVIRONMENT TIDY AND INVITING
- [ ] LISTENING TO SOFT MUSIC OR NATURE SOUNDS
- [ ] PULLING AN ORACLE CARD FOR INSPIRATION
- [ ] OTHER:_____

WHERE/WHEN DID I FEEL MOST INTUITIVE TODAY?

_____

_____

WHAT WAS MOST ENCOURAGING, COMFORTING, OR EXCITING ABOUT CONNECTING WITH MY INTUITION TODAY?

_____

_____

MORNING REFLECTION   DATE ___ / ___ / ___

HOW I'D RATE MY OPENNESS TO INTUITIVE GUIDANCE TODAY:

1   2   3   4   5   6   7   8   9   10

CLOSED/DISTRACTED   OPEN/GROUNDED

LAST NIGHT'S INTUITIVE DREAMS, OR INTUITIVE INSIGHTS WHEN I AWOKE:
_____
_____

TODAY I'D LIKE TO RECEIVE AN INTUITIVE SIGN ABOUT:
_____
_____

GOALS TO HELP ME FEEL LESS SCATTERED AND MORE CENTERED TODAY:
_____   _____
_____   _____

HOW I PLAN TO CONNECT MINDFULLY WITH MY INTUITION TODAY:
_____
_____
_____

MY MORNING INTUITIVE ROUTINE INCLUDED:

☐ MEDITATION   ☐ TIME IN NATURE   ☐ SELF-CARE:_____

☐ PRAYER   ☐ A HEALTHY BREAKFAST   ☐ OTHER:_____

☐ JOURNALING   ☐ SACRED PAUSES   _____

GUT CHECK—WHAT IS THE STRONGEST INSTINCT I HAVE RIGHT NOW ABOUT
HOW TO APPROACH A SITUATION, PERSON, OR ISSUE I'M FACING TODAY?
_____
_____
_____

EVENING REFLECTION

HOW I'D RATE MY ABILITY TO CONNECT WITH MY INTUITION TODAY:

1   2   3   4   5   6   7   8   9   10

DISCONNECTED   CONNECTED

MEANINGFUL COINCIDENCES, THEMES, OR PATTERNS I ENCOUNTERED TODAY:

_____

_____

_____

INTUITIVE INSIGHTS I EXPERIENCED INTERNALLY OR PHYSICALLY:

_____

_____

THINGS THAT CONNECTED ME TO MY INTUITION TODAY:

☐ GETTING QUALITY QUIET TIME OR TIME ALONE

☐ MINDFULLY SLOWING DOWN

☐ LOWERING MY STRESS LEVELS

☐ HAVING NOURISHING WORK AND HOME ROUTINES

☐ KEEPING MY ENVIRONMENT TIDY AND INVITING

☐ LISTENING TO SOFT MUSIC OR NATURE SOUNDS

☐ PULLING AN ORACLE CARD FOR INSPIRATION

☐ OTHER:_____

WHERE/WHEN DID I FEEL MOST INTUITIVE TODAY?

_____

_____

WHAT WAS MOST ENCOURAGING, COMFORTING, OR EXCITING ABOUT
CONNECTING WITH MY INTUITION TODAY?

_____

_____

MORNING REFLECTION

DATE ___/___/___

HOW I'D RATE MY OPENNESS TO INTUITIVE GUIDANCE TODAY:

1   2   3   4   5   6   7   8   9   10

CLOSED/DISTRACTED   OPEN/GROUNDED

LAST NIGHT'S INTUITIVE DREAMS, OR INTUITIVE INSIGHTS WHEN I AWOKE:
_____
_____

TODAY I'D LIKE TO RECEIVE AN INTUITIVE SIGN ABOUT:
_____
_____

GOALS TO HELP ME FEEL LESS SCATTERED AND MORE CENTERED TODAY:
_____   _____
_____   _____

HOW I PLAN TO CONNECT MINDFULLY WITH MY INTUITION TODAY:
_____
_____
_____

MY MORNING INTUITIVE ROUTINE INCLUDED:

☐ MEDITATION   ☐ TIME IN NATURE   ☐ SELF-CARE:_____
☐ PRAYER   ☐ A HEALTHY BREAKFAST   ☐ OTHER:_____
☐ JOURNALING   ☐ SACRED PAUSES   _____

GUT CHECK—WHAT IS THE STRONGEST INSTINCT I HAVE RIGHT NOW ABOUT HOW TO APPROACH A SITUATION, PERSON, OR ISSUE I'M FACING TODAY?
_____
_____

EVENING REFLECTION

HOW I'D RATE MY ABILITY TO CONNECT WITH MY INTUITION TODAY:

1	2	3	4	5	6	7	8	9	10

DISCONNECTED   CONNECTED

MEANINGFUL COINCIDENCES, THEMES, OR PATTERNS I ENCOUNTERED TODAY:
_____
_____
_____

INTUITIVE INSIGHTS I EXPERIENCED INTERNALLY OR PHYSICALLY:
_____
_____

THINGS THAT CONNECTED ME TO MY INTUITION TODAY:

- [ ] GETTING QUALITY QUIET TIME OR TIME ALONE
- [ ] MINDFULLY SLOWING DOWN
- [ ] LOWERING MY STRESS LEVELS
- [ ] HAVING NOURISHING WORK AND HOME ROUTINES
- [ ] KEEPING MY ENVIRONMENT TIDY AND INVITING
- [ ] LISTENING TO SOFT MUSIC OR NATURE SOUNDS
- [ ] PULLING AN ORACLE CARD FOR INSPIRATION
- [ ] OTHER:_____

WHERE/WHEN DID I FEEL MOST INTUITIVE TODAY?
_____
_____

WHAT WAS MOST ENCOURAGING, COMFORTING, OR EXCITING ABOUT
CONNECTING WITH MY INTUITION TODAY?
_____
_____

MORNING REFLECTION DATE ___/___/___

HOW I'D RATE MY OPENNESS TO INTUITIVE GUIDANCE TODAY:

1   2   3   4   5   6   7   8   9   10

CLOSED/DISTRACTED   OPEN/GROUNDED

LAST NIGHT'S INTUITIVE DREAMS, OR INTUITIVE INSIGHTS WHEN I AWOKE:

_____

_____

TODAY I'D LIKE TO RECEIVE AN INTUITIVE SIGN ABOUT:

_____

_____

GOALS TO HELP ME FEEL LESS SCATTERED AND MORE CENTERED TODAY:

_____   _____

_____   _____

HOW I PLAN TO CONNECT MINDFULLY WITH MY INTUITION TODAY:

_____

_____

_____

MY MORNING INTUITIVE ROUTINE INCLUDED:

☐ MEDITATION   ☐ TIME IN NATURE   ☐ SELF-CARE:_____

☐ PRAYER   ☐ A HEALTHY BREAKFAST   ☐ OTHER:_____

☐ JOURNALING   ☐ SACRED PAUSES   _____

GUT CHECK—WHAT IS THE STRONGEST INSTINCT I HAVE RIGHT NOW ABOUT
HOW TO APPROACH A SITUATION, PERSON, OR ISSUE I'M FACING TODAY?

_____

_____

_____

EVENING REFLECTION

HOW I'D RATE MY ABILITY TO CONNECT WITH MY INTUITION TODAY:

1	2	3	4	5	6	7	8	9	10

DISCONNECTED   CONNECTED

MEANINGFUL COINCIDENCES, THEMES, OR PATTERNS I ENCOUNTERED TODAY:
_____
_____
_____

INTUITIVE INSIGHTS I EXPERIENCED INTERNALLY OR PHYSICALLY:
_____
_____

THINGS THAT CONNECTED ME TO MY INTUITION TODAY:

☐ GETTING QUALITY QUIET TIME OR TIME ALONE

☐ MINDFULLY SLOWING DOWN

☐ LOWERING MY STRESS LEVELS

☐ HAVING NOURISHING WORK AND HOME ROUTINES

☐ KEEPING MY ENVIRONMENT TIDY AND INVITING

☐ LISTENING TO SOFT MUSIC OR NATURE SOUNDS

☐ PULLING AN ORACLE CARD FOR INSPIRATION

☐ OTHER:_____

WHERE/WHEN DID I FEEL MOST INTUITIVE TODAY?
_____
_____

WHAT WAS MOST ENCOURAGING, COMFORTING, OR EXCITING ABOUT
CONNECTING WITH MY INTUITION TODAY?
_____
_____

MORNING REFLECTION   DATE ___/___/___

HOW I'D RATE MY OPENNESS TO INTUITIVE GUIDANCE TODAY:

1   2   3   4   5   6   7   8   9   10

CLOSED/DISTRACTED   OPEN/GROUNDED

LAST NIGHT'S INTUITIVE DREAMS, OR INTUITIVE INSIGHTS WHEN I AWOKE:

_____

_____

TODAY I'D LIKE TO RECEIVE AN INTUITIVE SIGN ABOUT:

_____

_____

GOALS TO HELP ME FEEL LESS SCATTERED AND MORE CENTERED TODAY:

_____   _____

_____   _____

HOW I PLAN TO CONNECT MINDFULLY WITH MY INTUITION TODAY:

_____

_____

_____

MY MORNING INTUITIVE ROUTINE INCLUDED:

☐ MEDITATION   ☐ TIME IN NATURE   ☐ SELF-CARE:_____

☐ PRAYER   ☐ A HEALTHY BREAKFAST   ☐ OTHER:_____

☐ JOURNALING   ☐ SACRED PAUSES   _____

GUT CHECK—WHAT IS THE STRONGEST INSTINCT I HAVE RIGHT NOW ABOUT
HOW TO APPROACH A SITUATION, PERSON, OR ISSUE I'M FACING TODAY?

_____

_____

_____

EVENING REFLECTION

HOW I'D RATE MY ABILITY TO CONNECT WITH MY INTUITION TODAY:

1   2   3   4   5   6   7   8   9   10

DISCONNECTED   CONNECTED

MEANINGFUL COINCIDENCES, THEMES, OR PATTERNS I ENCOUNTERED TODAY:

_____

_____

_____

INTUITIVE INSIGHTS I EXPERIENCED INTERNALLY OR PHYSICALLY:

_____

_____

THINGS THAT CONNECTED ME TO MY INTUITION TODAY:

☐ GETTING QUALITY QUIET TIME OR TIME ALONE

☐ MINDFULLY SLOWING DOWN

☐ LOWERING MY STRESS LEVELS

☐ HAVING NOURISHING WORK AND HOME ROUTINES

☐ KEEPING MY ENVIRONMENT TIDY AND INVITING

☐ LISTENING TO SOFT MUSIC OR NATURE SOUNDS

☐ PULLING AN ORACLE CARD FOR INSPIRATION

☐ OTHER:_____

WHERE/WHEN DID I FEEL MOST INTUITIVE TODAY?

_____

_____

WHAT WAS MOST ENCOURAGING, COMFORTING, OR EXCITING ABOUT
CONNECTING WITH MY INTUITION TODAY?

_____

_____

MORNING REFLECTION

DATE ___/___/___

HOW I'D RATE MY OPENNESS TO INTUITIVE GUIDANCE TODAY:

1   2   3   4   5   6   7   8   9   10

CLOSED/DISTRACTED   OPEN/GROUNDED

LAST NIGHT'S INTUITIVE DREAMS, OR INTUITIVE INSIGHTS WHEN I AWOKE:

_____

_____

TODAY I'D LIKE TO RECEIVE AN INTUITIVE SIGN ABOUT:

_____

_____

GOALS TO HELP ME FEEL LESS SCATTERED AND MORE CENTERED TODAY:

_____   _____

_____   _____

HOW I PLAN TO CONNECT MINDFULLY WITH MY INTUITION TODAY:

_____

_____

_____

MY MORNING INTUITIVE ROUTINE INCLUDED:

☐ MEDITATION   ☐ TIME IN NATURE   ☐ SELF-CARE:_____

☐ PRAYER   ☐ A HEALTHY BREAKFAST   ☐ OTHER:_____

☐ JOURNALING   ☐ SACRED PAUSES   _____

GUT CHECK—WHAT IS THE STRONGEST INSTINCT I HAVE RIGHT NOW ABOUT
HOW TO APPROACH A SITUATION, PERSON, OR ISSUE I'M FACING TODAY?

_____

_____

_____

EVENING REFLECTION

HOW I'D RATE MY ABILITY TO CONNECT WITH MY INTUITION TODAY:

1   2   3   4   5   6   7   8   9   10

DISCONNECTED   CONNECTED

MEANINGFUL COINCIDENCES, THEMES, OR PATTERNS I ENCOUNTERED TODAY:

_____

_____

_____

INTUITIVE INSIGHTS I EXPERIENCED INTERNALLY OR PHYSICALLY:

_____

_____

THINGS THAT CONNECTED ME TO MY INTUITION TODAY:

- [ ] GETTING QUALITY QUIET TIME OR TIME ALONE
- [ ] MINDFULLY SLOWING DOWN
- [ ] LOWERING MY STRESS LEVELS
- [ ] HAVING NOURISHING WORK AND HOME ROUTINES
- [ ] KEEPING MY ENVIRONMENT TIDY AND INVITING
- [ ] LISTENING TO SOFT MUSIC OR NATURE SOUNDS
- [ ] PULLING AN ORACLE CARD FOR INSPIRATION
- [ ] OTHER: _____

WHERE/WHEN DID I FEEL MOST INTUITIVE TODAY?

_____

_____

WHAT WAS MOST ENCOURAGING, COMFORTING, OR EXCITING ABOUT
CONNECTING WITH MY INTUITION TODAY?

_____

_____

MORNING REFLECTION   DATE ___/___/___

HOW I'D RATE MY OPENNESS TO INTUITIVE GUIDANCE TODAY:

1   2   3   4   5   6   7   8   9   10

CLOSED/DISTRACTED   OPEN/GROUNDED

LAST NIGHT'S INTUITIVE DREAMS, OR INTUITIVE INSIGHTS WHEN I AWOKE:
_____
_____

TODAY I'D LIKE TO RECEIVE AN INTUITIVE SIGN ABOUT:
_____
_____

GOALS TO HELP ME FEEL LESS SCATTERED AND MORE CENTERED TODAY:
_____   _____
_____   _____

HOW I PLAN TO CONNECT MINDFULLY WITH MY INTUITION TODAY:
_____
_____
_____

MY MORNING INTUITIVE ROUTINE INCLUDED:

☐ MEDITATION   ☐ TIME IN NATURE   ☐ SELF-CARE:_____
☐ PRAYER   ☐ A HEALTHY BREAKFAST   ☐ OTHER:_____
☐ JOURNALING   ☐ SACRED PAUSES   _____

GUT CHECK—WHAT IS THE STRONGEST INSTINCT I HAVE RIGHT NOW ABOUT
HOW TO APPROACH A SITUATION, PERSON, OR ISSUE I'M FACING TODAY?
_____
_____
_____

EVENING REFLECTION

HOW I'D RATE MY ABILITY TO CONNECT WITH MY INTUITION TODAY:

1	2	3	4	5	6	7	8	9	10

DISCONNECTED   CONNECTED

MEANINGFUL COINCIDENCES, THEMES, OR PATTERNS I ENCOUNTERED TODAY:

_____

_____

_____

INTUITIVE INSIGHTS I EXPERIENCED INTERNALLY OR PHYSICALLY:

_____

_____

THINGS THAT CONNECTED ME TO MY INTUITION TODAY:

☐ GETTING QUALITY QUIET TIME OR TIME ALONE
☐ MINDFULLY SLOWING DOWN
☐ LOWERING MY STRESS LEVELS
☐ HAVING NOURISHING WORK AND HOME ROUTINES
☐ KEEPING MY ENVIRONMENT TIDY AND INVITING
☐ LISTENING TO SOFT MUSIC OR NATURE SOUNDS
☐ PULLING AN ORACLE CARD FOR INSPIRATION
☐ OTHER:_____

WHERE/WHEN DID I FEEL MOST INTUITIVE TODAY?

_____

_____

WHAT WAS MOST ENCOURAGING, COMFORTING, OR EXCITING ABOUT
CONNECTING WITH MY INTUITION TODAY?

_____

_____

MORNING REFLECTION DATE ___/___/___

HOW I'D RATE MY OPENNESS TO INTUITIVE GUIDANCE TODAY:

1   2   3   4   5   6   7   8   9   10

CLOSED/DISTRACTED   OPEN/GROUNDED

LAST NIGHT'S INTUITIVE DREAMS, OR INTUITIVE INSIGHTS WHEN I AWOKE:

_____

_____

TODAY I'D LIKE TO RECEIVE AN INTUITIVE SIGN ABOUT:

_____

_____

GOALS TO HELP ME FEEL LESS SCATTERED AND MORE CENTERED TODAY:

_____   _____

_____   _____

HOW I PLAN TO CONNECT MINDFULLY WITH MY INTUITION TODAY:

_____

_____

_____

MY MORNING INTUITIVE ROUTINE INCLUDED:

☐ MEDITATION   ☐ TIME IN NATURE   ☐ SELF-CARE:_____

☐ PRAYER   ☐ A HEALTHY BREAKFAST   ☐ OTHER:_____

☐ JOURNALING   ☐ SACRED PAUSES   _____

GUT CHECK—WHAT IS THE STRONGEST INSTINCT I HAVE RIGHT NOW ABOUT
HOW TO APPROACH A SITUATION, PERSON, OR ISSUE I'M FACING TODAY?

_____

_____

EVENING REFLECTION

HOW I'D RATE MY ABILITY TO CONNECT WITH MY INTUITION TODAY:

1   2   3   4   5   6   7   8   9   10
DISCONNECTED   CONNECTED

MEANINGFUL COINCIDENCES, THEMES, OR PATTERNS I ENCOUNTERED TODAY:

_____

_____

_____

INTUITIVE INSIGHTS I EXPERIENCED INTERNALLY OR PHYSICALLY:

_____

_____

THINGS THAT CONNECTED ME TO MY INTUITION TODAY:

☐ GETTING QUALITY QUIET TIME OR TIME ALONE

☐ MINDFULLY SLOWING DOWN

☐ LOWERING MY STRESS LEVELS

☐ HAVING NOURISHING WORK AND HOME ROUTINES

☐ KEEPING MY ENVIRONMENT TIDY AND INVITING

☐ LISTENING TO SOFT MUSIC OR NATURE SOUNDS

☐ PULLING AN ORACLE CARD FOR INSPIRATION

☐ OTHER:_____

WHERE/WHEN DID I FEEL MOST INTUITIVE TODAY?

_____

_____

WHAT WAS MOST ENCOURAGING, COMFORTING, OR EXCITING ABOUT
CONNECTING WITH MY INTUITION TODAY?

_____

_____

MORNING REFLECTION   DATE ___ / ___ / ___

HOW I'D RATE MY OPENNESS TO INTUITIVE GUIDANCE TODAY:

1   2   3   4   5   6   7   8   9   10

CLOSED/DISTRACTED   OPEN/GROUNDED

LAST NIGHT'S INTUITIVE DREAMS, OR INTUITIVE INSIGHTS WHEN I AWOKE:
_____
_____

TODAY I'D LIKE TO RECEIVE AN INTUITIVE SIGN ABOUT:
_____
_____

GOALS TO HELP ME FEEL LESS SCATTERED AND MORE CENTERED TODAY:
_____   _____
_____   _____

HOW I PLAN TO CONNECT MINDFULLY WITH MY INTUITION TODAY:
_____
_____
_____

MY MORNING INTUITIVE ROUTINE INCLUDED:

☐ MEDITATION   ☐ TIME IN NATURE   ☐ SELF-CARE:_____
☐ PRAYER   ☐ A HEALTHY BREAKFAST   ☐ OTHER:_____
☐ JOURNALING   ☐ SACRED PAUSES   _____

GUT CHECK—WHAT IS THE STRONGEST INSTINCT I HAVE RIGHT NOW ABOUT
HOW TO APPROACH A SITUATION, PERSON, OR ISSUE I'M FACING TODAY?
_____
_____
_____

EVENING REFLECTION

HOW I'D RATE MY ABILITY TO CONNECT WITH MY INTUITION TODAY:

1   2   3   4   5   6   7   8   9   10

DISCONNECTED   CONNECTED

MEANINGFUL COINCIDENCES, THEMES, OR PATTERNS I ENCOUNTERED TODAY:

_____

_____

_____

INTUITIVE INSIGHTS I EXPERIENCED INTERNALLY OR PHYSICALLY:

_____

_____

THINGS THAT CONNECTED ME TO MY INTUITION TODAY:

☐ GETTING QUALITY QUIET TIME OR TIME ALONE

☐ MINDFULLY SLOWING DOWN

☐ LOWERING MY STRESS LEVELS

☐ HAVING NOURISHING WORK AND HOME ROUTINES

☐ KEEPING MY ENVIRONMENT TIDY AND INVITING

☐ LISTENING TO SOFT MUSIC OR NATURE SOUNDS

☐ PULLING AN ORACLE CARD FOR INSPIRATION

☐ OTHER:_____

WHERE/WHEN DID I FEEL MOST INTUITIVE TODAY?

_____

_____

WHAT WAS MOST ENCOURAGING, COMFORTING, OR EXCITING ABOUT
CONNECTING WITH MY INTUITION TODAY?

_____

_____

MORNING REFLECTION
DATE ___/___/___

HOW I'D RATE MY OPENNESS TO INTUITIVE GUIDANCE TODAY:

1   2   3   4   5   6   7   8   9   10

CLOSED/DISTRACTED   OPEN/GROUNDED

LAST NIGHT'S INTUITIVE DREAMS, OR INTUITIVE INSIGHTS WHEN I AWOKE:
_____
_____

TODAY I'D LIKE TO RECEIVE AN INTUITIVE SIGN ABOUT:
_____
_____

GOALS TO HELP ME FEEL LESS SCATTERED AND MORE CENTERED TODAY:
_____   _____
_____   _____

HOW I PLAN TO CONNECT MINDFULLY WITH MY INTUITION TODAY:
_____
_____
_____

MY MORNING INTUITIVE ROUTINE INCLUDED:

☐ MEDITATION   ☐ TIME IN NATURE   ☐ SELF-CARE:_____
☐ PRAYER   ☐ A HEALTHY BREAKFAST   ☐ OTHER:_____
☐ JOURNALING   ☐ SACRED PAUSES   _____

GUT CHECK—WHAT IS THE STRONGEST INSTINCT I HAVE RIGHT NOW ABOUT
HOW TO APPROACH A SITUATION, PERSON, OR ISSUE I'M FACING TODAY?
_____
_____
_____

EVENING REFLECTION

HOW I'D RATE MY ABILITY TO CONNECT WITH MY INTUITION TODAY:

1	2	3	4	5	6	7	8	9	10

DISCONNECTED   CONNECTED

MEANINGFUL COINCIDENCES, THEMES, OR PATTERNS I ENCOUNTERED TODAY:
_____
_____
_____

INTUITIVE INSIGHTS I EXPERIENCED INTERNALLY OR PHYSICALLY:
_____
_____

THINGS THAT CONNECTED ME TO MY INTUITION TODAY:

☐ GETTING QUALITY QUIET TIME OR TIME ALONE
☐ MINDFULLY SLOWING DOWN
☐ LOWERING MY STRESS LEVELS
☐ HAVING NOURISHING WORK AND HOME ROUTINES
☐ KEEPING MY ENVIRONMENT TIDY AND INVITING
☐ LISTENING TO SOFT MUSIC OR NATURE SOUNDS
☐ PULLING AN ORACLE CARD FOR INSPIRATION
☐ OTHER:_____

WHERE/WHEN DID I FEEL MOST INTUITIVE TODAY?
_____
_____

WHAT WAS MOST ENCOURAGING, COMFORTING, OR EXCITING ABOUT
CONNECTING WITH MY INTUITION TODAY?
_____
_____

MORNING REFLECTION   DATE ___ / ___ / ___

HOW I'D RATE MY OPENNESS TO INTUITIVE GUIDANCE TODAY:

1   2   3   4   5   6   7   8   9   10
CLOSED/DISTRACTED   OPEN/GROUNDED

LAST NIGHT'S INTUITIVE DREAMS, OR INTUITIVE INSIGHTS WHEN I AWOKE:
_____
_____

TODAY I'D LIKE TO RECEIVE AN INTUITIVE SIGN ABOUT:
_____
_____

GOALS TO HELP ME FEEL LESS SCATTERED AND MORE CENTERED TODAY:
_____   _____
_____   _____

HOW I PLAN TO CONNECT MINDFULLY WITH MY INTUITION TODAY:
_____
_____
_____

MY MORNING INTUITIVE ROUTINE INCLUDED:

☐ MEDITATION   ☐ TIME IN NATURE   ☐ SELF-CARE:_____
☐ PRAYER   ☐ A HEALTHY BREAKFAST   ☐ OTHER:_____
☐ JOURNALING   ☐ SACRED PAUSES   _____

GUT CHECK—WHAT IS THE STRONGEST INSTINCT I HAVE RIGHT NOW ABOUT
HOW TO APPROACH A SITUATION, PERSON, OR ISSUE I'M FACING TODAY?
_____
_____
_____

EVENING REFLECTION

HOW I'D RATE MY ABILITY TO CONNECT WITH MY INTUITION TODAY:

1   2   3   4   5   6   7   8   9   10

DISCONNECTED   CONNECTED

MEANINGFUL COINCIDENCES, THEMES, OR PATTERNS I ENCOUNTERED TODAY:

_____

_____

_____

INTUITIVE INSIGHTS I EXPERIENCED INTERNALLY OR PHYSICALLY:

_____

_____

THINGS THAT CONNECTED ME TO MY INTUITION TODAY:

☐ GETTING QUALITY QUIET TIME OR TIME ALONE

☐ MINDFULLY SLOWING DOWN

☐ LOWERING MY STRESS LEVELS

☐ HAVING NOURISHING WORK AND HOME ROUTINES

☐ KEEPING MY ENVIRONMENT TIDY AND INVITING

☐ LISTENING TO SOFT MUSIC OR NATURE SOUNDS

☐ PULLING AN ORACLE CARD FOR INSPIRATION

☐ OTHER:_____

WHERE/WHEN DID I FEEL MOST INTUITIVE TODAY?

_____

_____

WHAT WAS MOST ENCOURAGING, COMFORTING, OR EXCITING ABOUT
CONNECTING WITH MY INTUITION TODAY?

_____

_____

MORNING REFLECTION

DATE ___ / ___ / ___

HOW I'D RATE MY OPENNESS TO INTUITIVE GUIDANCE TODAY:

1	2	3	4	5	6	7	8	9	10

CLOSED/DISTRACTED   OPEN/GROUNDED

LAST NIGHT'S INTUITIVE DREAMS, OR INTUITIVE INSIGHTS WHEN I AWOKE:

_____

_____

TODAY I'D LIKE TO RECEIVE AN INTUITIVE SIGN ABOUT:

_____

_____

GOALS TO HELP ME FEEL LESS SCATTERED AND MORE CENTERED TODAY:

_____   _____

_____   _____

HOW I PLAN TO CONNECT MINDFULLY WITH MY INTUITION TODAY:

_____

_____

_____

MY MORNING INTUITIVE ROUTINE INCLUDED:

☐ MEDITATION   ☐ TIME IN NATURE   ☐ SELF-CARE:_____

☐ PRAYER   ☐ A HEALTHY BREAKFAST   ☐ OTHER:_____

☐ JOURNALING   ☐ SACRED PAUSES   _____

GUT CHECK—WHAT IS THE STRONGEST INSTINCT I HAVE RIGHT NOW ABOUT
HOW TO APPROACH A SITUATION, PERSON, OR ISSUE I'M FACING TODAY?

_____

_____

_____

EVENING REFLECTION

HOW I'D RATE MY ABILITY TO CONNECT WITH MY INTUITION TODAY:

1   2   3   4   5   6   7   8   9   10

DISCONNECTED   CONNECTED

MEANINGFUL COINCIDENCES, THEMES, OR PATTERNS I ENCOUNTERED TODAY:

_____

_____

_____

INTUITIVE INSIGHTS I EXPERIENCED INTERNALLY OR PHYSICALLY:

_____

_____

THINGS THAT CONNECTED ME TO MY INTUITION TODAY:

☐ GETTING QUALITY QUIET TIME OR TIME ALONE

☐ MINDFULLY SLOWING DOWN

☐ LOWERING MY STRESS LEVELS

☐ HAVING NOURISHING WORK AND HOME ROUTINES

☐ KEEPING MY ENVIRONMENT TIDY AND INVITING

☐ LISTENING TO SOFT MUSIC OR NATURE SOUNDS

☐ PULLING AN ORACLE CARD FOR INSPIRATION

☐ OTHER:_____

WHERE/WHEN DID I FEEL MOST INTUITIVE TODAY?

_____

_____

WHAT WAS MOST ENCOURAGING, COMFORTING, OR EXCITING ABOUT
CONNECTING WITH MY INTUITION TODAY?

_____

_____

MORNING REFLECTION

DATE ___/___/___

HOW I'D RATE MY OPENNESS TO INTUITIVE GUIDANCE TODAY:

1   2   3   4   5   6   7   8   9   10

CLOSED/DISTRACTED   OPEN/GROUNDED

LAST NIGHT'S INTUITIVE DREAMS, OR INTUITIVE INSIGHTS WHEN I AWOKE:

_____

_____

TODAY I'D LIKE TO RECEIVE AN INTUITIVE SIGN ABOUT:

_____

_____

GOALS TO HELP ME FEEL LESS SCATTERED AND MORE CENTERED TODAY:

_____   _____

_____   _____

HOW I PLAN TO CONNECT MINDFULLY WITH MY INTUITION TODAY:

_____

_____

_____

MY MORNING INTUITIVE ROUTINE INCLUDED:

☐ MEDITATION   ☐ TIME IN NATURE   ☐ SELF-CARE:_____

☐ PRAYER   ☐ A HEALTHY BREAKFAST   ☐ OTHER:_____

☐ JOURNALING   ☐ SACRED PAUSES   _____

GUT CHECK—WHAT IS THE STRONGEST INSTINCT I HAVE RIGHT NOW ABOUT
HOW TO APPROACH A SITUATION, PERSON, OR ISSUE I'M FACING TODAY?

_____

_____

_____

EVENING REFLECTION

HOW I'D RATE MY ABILITY TO CONNECT WITH MY INTUITION TODAY:

1   2   3   4   5   6   7   8   9   10

DISCONNECTED   CONNECTED

MEANINGFUL COINCIDENCES, THEMES, OR PATTERNS I ENCOUNTERED TODAY:

_____

_____

_____

INTUITIVE INSIGHTS I EXPERIENCED INTERNALLY OR PHYSICALLY:

_____

_____

THINGS THAT CONNECTED ME TO MY INTUITION TODAY:

☐ GETTING QUALITY QUIET TIME OR TIME ALONE

☐ MINDFULLY SLOWING DOWN

☐ LOWERING MY STRESS LEVELS

☐ HAVING NOURISHING WORK AND HOME ROUTINES

☐ KEEPING MY ENVIRONMENT TIDY AND INVITING

☐ LISTENING TO SOFT MUSIC OR NATURE SOUNDS

☐ PULLING AN ORACLE CARD FOR INSPIRATION

☐ OTHER:_____

WHERE/WHEN DID I FEEL MOST INTUITIVE TODAY?

_____

_____

WHAT WAS MOST ENCOURAGING, COMFORTING, OR EXCITING ABOUT
CONNECTING WITH MY INTUITION TODAY?

_____

_____

MORNING REFLECTION DATE ___/___/___

LAST NIGHT'S INTUITIVE DREAMS, OR INTUITIVE INSIGHTS WHEN I AWOKE:

_____

_____

TODAY I'D LIKE TO RECEIVE AN INTUITIVE SIGN ABOUT:

_____

_____

GOALS TO HELP ME FEEL LESS SCATTERED AND MORE CENTERED TODAY:

_____   _____

_____   _____

HOW I PLAN TO CONNECT MINDFULLY WITH MY INTUITION TODAY:

_____

_____

_____

MY MORNING INTUITIVE ROUTINE INCLUDED:

☐ MEDITATION   ☐ TIME IN NATURE   ☐ SELF-CARE:_____

☐ PRAYER   ☐ A HEALTHY BREAKFAST   ☐ OTHER:_____

☐ JOURNALING   ☐ SACRED PAUSES   _____

GUT CHECK—WHAT IS THE STRONGEST INSTINCT I HAVE RIGHT NOW ABOUT
HOW TO APPROACH A SITUATION, PERSON, OR ISSUE I'M FACING TODAY?

_____

_____

_____

EVENING REFLECTION

HOW I'D RATE MY ABILITY TO CONNECT WITH MY INTUITION TODAY:

1   2   3   4   5   6   7   8   9   10

DISCONNECTED   CONNECTED

MEANINGFUL COINCIDENCES, THEMES, OR PATTERNS I ENCOUNTERED TODAY:

_____

_____

_____

INTUITIVE INSIGHTS I EXPERIENCED INTERNALLY OR PHYSICALLY:

_____

_____

THINGS THAT CONNECTED ME TO MY INTUITION TODAY:

☐ GETTING QUALITY QUIET TIME OR TIME ALONE

☐ MINDFULLY SLOWING DOWN

☐ LOWERING MY STRESS LEVELS

☐ HAVING NOURISHING WORK AND HOME ROUTINES

☐ KEEPING MY ENVIRONMENT TIDY AND INVITING

☐ LISTENING TO SOFT MUSIC OR NATURE SOUNDS

☐ PULLING AN ORACLE CARD FOR INSPIRATION

☐ OTHER:_____

WHERE/WHEN DID I FEEL MOST INTUITIVE TODAY?

_____

_____

WHAT WAS MOST ENCOURAGING, COMFORTING, OR EXCITING ABOUT
CONNECTING WITH MY INTUITION TODAY?

_____

_____

MORNING REFLECTION   DATE ___/___/___

HOW I'D RATE MY OPENNESS TO INTUITIVE GUIDANCE TODAY:

1   2   3   4   5   6   7   8   9   10

CLOSED/DISTRACTED   OPEN/GROUNDED

LAST NIGHT'S INTUITIVE DREAMS, OR INTUITIVE INSIGHTS WHEN I AWOKE:
_____
_____

TODAY I'D LIKE TO RECEIVE AN INTUITIVE SIGN ABOUT:
_____
_____

GOALS TO HELP ME FEEL LESS SCATTERED AND MORE CENTERED TODAY:
_____   _____
_____   _____

HOW I PLAN TO CONNECT MINDFULLY WITH MY INTUITION TODAY:
_____
_____
_____

MY MORNING INTUITIVE ROUTINE INCLUDED:

☐ MEDITATION   ☐ TIME IN NATURE   ☐ SELF-CARE:_____
☐ PRAYER   ☐ A HEALTHY BREAKFAST   ☐ OTHER:_____
☐ JOURNALING   ☐ SACRED PAUSES   _____

GUT CHECK—WHAT IS THE STRONGEST INSTINCT I HAVE RIGHT NOW ABOUT
HOW TO APPROACH A SITUATION, PERSON, OR ISSUE I'M FACING TODAY?
_____
_____
_____

EVENING REFLECTION

HOW I'D RATE MY ABILITY TO CONNECT WITH MY INTUITION TODAY:

1   2   3   4   5   6   7   8   9   10

DISCONNECTED   CONNECTED

MEANINGFUL COINCIDENCES, THEMES, OR PATTERNS I ENCOUNTERED TODAY:

_____

_____

_____

INTUITIVE INSIGHTS I EXPERIENCED INTERNALLY OR PHYSICALLY:

_____

_____

THINGS THAT CONNECTED ME TO MY INTUITION TODAY:

☐ GETTING QUALITY QUIET TIME OR TIME ALONE

☐ MINDFULLY SLOWING DOWN

☐ LOWERING MY STRESS LEVELS

☐ HAVING NOURISHING WORK AND HOME ROUTINES

☐ KEEPING MY ENVIRONMENT TIDY AND INVITING

☐ LISTENING TO SOFT MUSIC OR NATURE SOUNDS

☐ PULLING AN ORACLE CARD FOR INSPIRATION

☐ OTHER:_____

WHERE/WHEN DID I FEEL MOST INTUITIVE TODAY?

_____

_____

WHAT WAS MOST ENCOURAGING, COMFORTING, OR EXCITING ABOUT
CONNECTING WITH MY INTUITION TODAY?

_____

_____

MORNING REFLECTION
DATE ___/___/___

HOW I'D RATE MY OPENNESS TO INTUITIVE GUIDANCE TODAY:

1   2   3   4   5   6   7   8   9   10

CLOSED/DISTRACTED   OPEN/GROUNDED

LAST NIGHT'S INTUITIVE DREAMS, OR INTUITIVE INSIGHTS WHEN I AWOKE:
_____
_____

TODAY I'D LIKE TO RECEIVE AN INTUITIVE SIGN ABOUT:
_____
_____

GOALS TO HELP ME FEEL LESS SCATTERED AND MORE CENTERED TODAY:
_____   _____
_____   _____

HOW I PLAN TO CONNECT MINDFULLY WITH MY INTUITION TODAY:
_____
_____
_____

MY MORNING INTUITIVE ROUTINE INCLUDED:

☐ MEDITATION   ☐ TIME IN NATURE   ☐ SELF-CARE:_____
☐ PRAYER   ☐ A HEALTHY BREAKFAST   ☐ OTHER:_____
☐ JOURNALING   ☐ SACRED PAUSES   _____

GUT CHECK—WHAT IS THE STRONGEST INSTINCT I HAVE RIGHT NOW ABOUT
HOW TO APPROACH A SITUATION, PERSON, OR ISSUE I'M FACING TODAY?
_____
_____
_____

EVENING REFLECTION

HOW I'D RATE MY ABILITY TO CONNECT WITH MY INTUITION TODAY:

1	2	3	4	5	6	7	8	9	10

DISCONNECTED   CONNECTED

MEANINGFUL COINCIDENCES, THEMES, OR PATTERNS I ENCOUNTERED TODAY:
_____
_____
_____

INTUITIVE INSIGHTS I EXPERIENCED INTERNALLY OR PHYSICALLY:
_____
_____

THINGS THAT CONNECTED ME TO MY INTUITION TODAY:

☐ GETTING QUALITY QUIET TIME OR TIME ALONE
☐ MINDFULLY SLOWING DOWN
☐ LOWERING MY STRESS LEVELS
☐ HAVING NOURISHING WORK AND HOME ROUTINES
☐ KEEPING MY ENVIRONMENT TIDY AND INVITING
☐ LISTENING TO SOFT MUSIC OR NATURE SOUNDS
☐ PULLING AN ORACLE CARD FOR INSPIRATION
☐ OTHER:_____

WHERE/WHEN DID I FEEL MOST INTUITIVE TODAY?
_____
_____

WHAT WAS MOST ENCOURAGING, COMFORTING, OR EXCITING ABOUT
CONNECTING WITH MY INTUITION TODAY?
_____
_____

MORNING REFLECTION

DATE ___ / ___ / ___

HOW I'D RATE MY OPENNESS TO INTUITIVE GUIDANCE TODAY:

1   2   3   4   5   6   7   8   9   10

CLOSED/DISTRACTED   OPEN/GROUNDED

LAST NIGHT'S INTUITIVE DREAMS, OR INTUITIVE INSIGHTS WHEN I AWOKE:

_____

_____

TODAY I'D LIKE TO RECEIVE AN INTUITIVE SIGN ABOUT:

_____

_____

GOALS TO HELP ME FEEL LESS SCATTERED AND MORE CENTERED TODAY:

_____   _____

_____   _____

HOW I PLAN TO CONNECT MINDFULLY WITH MY INTUITION TODAY:

_____

_____

_____

MY MORNING INTUITIVE ROUTINE INCLUDED:

☐ MEDITATION   ☐ TIME IN NATURE   ☐ SELF-CARE:_____

☐ PRAYER   ☐ A HEALTHY BREAKFAST   ☐ OTHER:_____

☐ JOURNALING   ☐ SACRED PAUSES   _____

GUT CHECK—WHAT IS THE STRONGEST INSTINCT I HAVE RIGHT NOW ABOUT
HOW TO APPROACH A SITUATION, PERSON, OR ISSUE I'M FACING TODAY?

_____

_____

_____

EVENING REFLECTION

HOW I'D RATE MY ABILITY TO CONNECT WITH MY INTUITION TODAY:

1   2   3   4   5   6   7   8   9   10

DISCONNECTED   CONNECTED

MEANINGFUL COINCIDENCES, THEMES, OR PATTERNS I ENCOUNTERED TODAY:

_____

_____

_____

INTUITIVE INSIGHTS I EXPERIENCED INTERNALLY OR PHYSICALLY:

_____

_____

THINGS THAT CONNECTED ME TO MY INTUITION TODAY:

☐ GETTING QUALITY QUIET TIME OR TIME ALONE

☐ MINDFULLY SLOWING DOWN

☐ LOWERING MY STRESS LEVELS

☐ HAVING NOURISHING WORK AND HOME ROUTINES

☐ KEEPING MY ENVIRONMENT TIDY AND INVITING

☐ LISTENING TO SOFT MUSIC OR NATURE SOUNDS

☐ PULLING AN ORACLE CARD FOR INSPIRATION

☐ OTHER:_____

WHERE/WHEN DID I FEEL MOST INTUITIVE TODAY?

_____

_____

WHAT WAS MOST ENCOURAGING, COMFORTING, OR EXCITING ABOUT
CONNECTING WITH MY INTUITION TODAY?

_____

_____

MORNING REFLECTION

DATE ___/___/___

HOW I'D RATE MY OPENNESS TO INTUITIVE GUIDANCE TODAY:

1	2	3	4	5	6	7	8	9	10

CLOSED/DISTRACTED   OPEN/GROUNDED

LAST NIGHT'S INTUITIVE DREAMS, OR INTUITIVE INSIGHTS WHEN I AWOKE:

_____

_____

TODAY I'D LIKE TO RECEIVE AN INTUITIVE SIGN ABOUT:

_____

_____

GOALS TO HELP ME FEEL LESS SCATTERED AND MORE CENTERED TODAY:

_____   _____

_____   _____

HOW I PLAN TO CONNECT MINDFULLY WITH MY INTUITION TODAY:

_____

_____

_____

MY MORNING INTUITIVE ROUTINE INCLUDED:

☐ MEDITATION   ☐ TIME IN NATURE   ☐ SELF-CARE:_____

☐ PRAYER   ☐ A HEALTHY BREAKFAST   ☐ OTHER:_____

☐ JOURNALING   ☐ SACRED PAUSES   _____

GUT CHECK—WHAT IS THE STRONGEST INSTINCT I HAVE RIGHT NOW ABOUT
HOW TO APPROACH A SITUATION, PERSON, OR ISSUE I'M FACING TODAY?

_____

_____

_____

EVENING REFLECTION

HOW I'D RATE MY ABILITY TO CONNECT WITH MY INTUITION TODAY:

1   2   3   4   5   6   7   8   9   10

DISCONNECTED   CONNECTED

MEANINGFUL COINCIDENCES, THEMES, OR PATTERNS I ENCOUNTERED TODAY:

_____

_____

_____

INTUITIVE INSIGHTS I EXPERIENCED INTERNALLY OR PHYSICALLY:

_____

_____

THINGS THAT CONNECTED ME TO MY INTUITION TODAY:

☐ GETTING QUALITY QUIET TIME OR TIME ALONE

☐ MINDFULLY SLOWING DOWN

☐ LOWERING MY STRESS LEVELS

☐ HAVING NOURISHING WORK AND HOME ROUTINES

☐ KEEPING MY ENVIRONMENT TIDY AND INVITING

☐ LISTENING TO SOFT MUSIC OR NATURE SOUNDS

☐ PULLING AN ORACLE CARD FOR INSPIRATION

☐ OTHER:_____

WHERE/WHEN DID I FEEL MOST INTUITIVE TODAY?

_____

_____

WHAT WAS MOST ENCOURAGING, COMFORTING, OR EXCITING ABOUT
CONNECTING WITH MY INTUITION TODAY?

_____

_____

MORNING REFLECTION DATE ___/___/___

HOW I'D RATE MY OPENNESS TO INTUITIVE GUIDANCE TODAY:

1   2   3   4   5   6   7   8   9   10

CLOSED/DISTRACTED   OPEN/GROUNDED

LAST NIGHT'S INTUITIVE DREAMS, OR INTUITIVE INSIGHTS WHEN I AWOKE:
_____
_____

TODAY I'D LIKE TO RECEIVE AN INTUITIVE SIGN ABOUT:
_____
_____

GOALS TO HELP ME FEEL LESS SCATTERED AND MORE CENTERED TODAY:
_____   _____
_____   _____

HOW I PLAN TO CONNECT MINDFULLY WITH MY INTUITION TODAY:
_____
_____
_____

MY MORNING INTUITIVE ROUTINE INCLUDED:

☐ MEDITATION   ☐ TIME IN NATURE   ☐ SELF-CARE:_____
☐ PRAYER   ☐ A HEALTHY BREAKFAST   ☐ OTHER:_____
☐ JOURNALING   ☐ SACRED PAUSES   _____

GUT CHECK—WHAT IS THE STRONGEST INSTINCT I HAVE RIGHT NOW ABOUT
HOW TO APPROACH A SITUATION, PERSON, OR ISSUE I'M FACING TODAY?
_____
_____
_____

EVENING REFLECTION

HOW I'D RATE MY ABILITY TO CONNECT WITH MY INTUITION TODAY:

| 1 | 2 | 3 | 4 | 5 | 6 | 7 | 8 | 9 | 10 |

DISCONNECTED   CONNECTED

MEANINGFUL COINCIDENCES, THEMES, OR PATTERNS I ENCOUNTERED TODAY:

_____

_____

_____

INTUITIVE INSIGHTS I EXPERIENCED INTERNALLY OR PHYSICALLY:

_____

_____

THINGS THAT CONNECTED ME TO MY INTUITION TODAY:

☐ GETTING QUALITY QUIET TIME OR TIME ALONE

☐ MINDFULLY SLOWING DOWN

☐ LOWERING MY STRESS LEVELS

☐ HAVING NOURISHING WORK AND HOME ROUTINES

☐ KEEPING MY ENVIRONMENT TIDY AND INVITING

☐ LISTENING TO SOFT MUSIC OR NATURE SOUNDS

☐ PULLING AN ORACLE CARD FOR INSPIRATION

☐ OTHER:_____

WHERE/WHEN DID I FEEL MOST INTUITIVE TODAY?

_____

_____

WHAT WAS MOST ENCOURAGING, COMFORTING, OR EXCITING ABOUT
CONNECTING WITH MY INTUITION TODAY?

_____

_____

MORNING REFLECTION DATE ___/___/___

LAST NIGHT'S INTUITIVE DREAMS, OR INTUITIVE INSIGHTS WHEN I AWOKE:

_____

_____

TODAY I'D LIKE TO RECEIVE AN INTUITIVE SIGN ABOUT:

_____

_____

GOALS TO HELP ME FEEL LESS SCATTERED AND MORE CENTERED TODAY:

_____   _____

_____   _____

HOW I PLAN TO CONNECT MINDFULLY WITH MY INTUITION TODAY:

_____

_____

_____

MY MORNING INTUITIVE ROUTINE INCLUDED:

☐ MEDITATION   ☐ TIME IN NATURE   ☐ SELF-CARE:_____

☐ PRAYER   ☐ A HEALTHY BREAKFAST   ☐ OTHER:_____

☐ JOURNALING   ☐ SACRED PAUSES   _____

GUT CHECK—WHAT IS THE STRONGEST INSTINCT I HAVE RIGHT NOW ABOUT
HOW TO APPROACH A SITUATION, PERSON, OR ISSUE I'M FACING TODAY?

_____

_____

_____

EVENING REFLECTION

HOW I'D RATE MY ABILITY TO CONNECT WITH MY INTUITION TODAY:

1   2   3   4   5   6   7   8   9   10

DISCONNECTED   CONNECTED

MEANINGFUL COINCIDENCES, THEMES, OR PATTERNS I ENCOUNTERED TODAY:

_____

_____

_____

INTUITIVE INSIGHTS I EXPERIENCED INTERNALLY OR PHYSICALLY:

_____

_____

THINGS THAT CONNECTED ME TO MY INTUITION TODAY:

☐ GETTING QUALITY QUIET TIME OR TIME ALONE

☐ MINDFULLY SLOWING DOWN

☐ LOWERING MY STRESS LEVELS

☐ HAVING NOURISHING WORK AND HOME ROUTINES

☐ KEEPING MY ENVIRONMENT TIDY AND INVITING

☐ LISTENING TO SOFT MUSIC OR NATURE SOUNDS

☐ PULLING AN ORACLE CARD FOR INSPIRATION

☐ OTHER:_____

WHERE/WHEN DID I FEEL MOST INTUITIVE TODAY?

_____

_____

WHAT WAS MOST ENCOURAGING, COMFORTING, OR EXCITING ABOUT
CONNECTING WITH MY INTUITION TODAY?

_____

_____

MORNING REFLECTION   DATE ___/___/___

HOW I'D RATE MY OPENNESS TO INTUITIVE GUIDANCE TODAY:

1   2   3   4   5   6   7   8   9   10

CLOSED/DISTRACTED   OPEN/GROUNDED

LAST NIGHT'S INTUITIVE DREAMS, OR INTUITIVE INSIGHTS WHEN I AWOKE:

_____

_____

TODAY I'D LIKE TO RECEIVE AN INTUITIVE SIGN ABOUT:

_____

_____

GOALS TO HELP ME FEEL LESS SCATTERED AND MORE CENTERED TODAY:

_____   _____

_____   _____

HOW I PLAN TO CONNECT MINDFULLY WITH MY INTUITION TODAY:

_____

_____

_____

MY MORNING INTUITIVE ROUTINE INCLUDED:

☐ MEDITATION   ☐ TIME IN NATURE   ☐ SELF-CARE:_____
☐ PRAYER   ☐ A HEALTHY BREAKFAST   ☐ OTHER:_____
☐ JOURNALING   ☐ SACRED PAUSES   _____

GUT CHECK—WHAT IS THE STRONGEST INSTINCT I HAVE RIGHT NOW ABOUT
HOW TO APPROACH A SITUATION, PERSON, OR ISSUE I'M FACING TODAY?

_____

_____

_____

EVENING REFLECTION

HOW I'D RATE MY ABILITY TO CONNECT WITH MY INTUITION TODAY:

1   2   3   4   5   6   7   8   9   10

DISCONNECTED   CONNECTED

MEANINGFUL COINCIDENCES, THEMES, OR PATTERNS I ENCOUNTERED TODAY:

_____

_____

_____

INTUITIVE INSIGHTS I EXPERIENCED INTERNALLY OR PHYSICALLY:

_____

_____

THINGS THAT CONNECTED ME TO MY INTUITION TODAY:

☐ GETTING QUALITY QUIET TIME OR TIME ALONE

☐ MINDFULLY SLOWING DOWN

☐ LOWERING MY STRESS LEVELS

☐ HAVING NOURISHING WORK AND HOME ROUTINES

☐ KEEPING MY ENVIRONMENT TIDY AND INVITING

☐ LISTENING TO SOFT MUSIC OR NATURE SOUNDS

☐ PULLING AN ORACLE CARD FOR INSPIRATION

☐ OTHER:_____

WHERE/WHEN DID I FEEL MOST INTUITIVE TODAY?

_____

_____

WHAT WAS MOST ENCOURAGING, COMFORTING, OR EXCITING ABOUT
CONNECTING WITH MY INTUITION TODAY?

_____

_____

MORNING REFLECTION DATE ___/___/___

HOW I'D RATE MY OPENNESS TO INTUITIVE GUIDANCE TODAY:

1   2   3   4   5   6   7   8   9   10

CLOSED/DISTRACTED   OPEN/GROUNDED

LAST NIGHT'S INTUITIVE DREAMS, OR INTUITIVE INSIGHTS WHEN I AWOKE:

_____

_____

TODAY I'D LIKE TO RECEIVE AN INTUITIVE SIGN ABOUT:

_____

_____

GOALS TO HELP ME FEEL LESS SCATTERED AND MORE CENTERED TODAY:

_____   _____

_____   _____

HOW I PLAN TO CONNECT MINDFULLY WITH MY INTUITION TODAY:

_____

_____

_____

MY MORNING INTUITIVE ROUTINE INCLUDED:

☐ MEDITATION   ☐ TIME IN NATURE   ☐ SELF-CARE:_____

☐ PRAYER   ☐ A HEALTHY BREAKFAST   ☐ OTHER:_____

☐ JOURNALING   ☐ SACRED PAUSES   _____

GUT CHECK—WHAT IS THE STRONGEST INSTINCT I HAVE RIGHT NOW ABOUT
HOW TO APPROACH A SITUATION, PERSON, OR ISSUE I'M FACING TODAY?

_____

_____

_____

EVENING REFLECTION

HOW I'D RATE MY ABILITY TO CONNECT WITH MY INTUITION TODAY:

1   2   3   4   5   6   7   8   9   10

DISCONNECTED   CONNECTED

MEANINGFUL COINCIDENCES, THEMES, OR PATTERNS I ENCOUNTERED TODAY:
_____
_____
_____

INTUITIVE INSIGHTS I EXPERIENCED INTERNALLY OR PHYSICALLY:
_____
_____

THINGS THAT CONNECTED ME TO MY INTUITION TODAY:

☐ GETTING QUALITY QUIET TIME OR TIME ALONE

☐ MINDFULLY SLOWING DOWN

☐ LOWERING MY STRESS LEVELS

☐ HAVING NOURISHING WORK AND HOME ROUTINES

☐ KEEPING MY ENVIRONMENT TIDY AND INVITING

☐ LISTENING TO SOFT MUSIC OR NATURE SOUNDS

☐ PULLING AN ORACLE CARD FOR INSPIRATION

☐ OTHER:_____

WHERE/WHEN DID I FEEL MOST INTUITIVE TODAY?
_____
_____

WHAT WAS MOST ENCOURAGING, COMFORTING, OR EXCITING ABOUT
CONNECTING WITH MY INTUITION TODAY?
_____
_____

MORNING REFLECTION

DATE ___/___/___

HOW I'D RATE MY OPENNESS TO INTUITIVE GUIDANCE TODAY:

1   2   3   4   5   6   7   8   9   10

CLOSED/DISTRACTED   OPEN/GROUNDED

LAST NIGHT'S INTUITIVE DREAMS, OR INTUITIVE INSIGHTS WHEN I AWOKE:

_____
_____

TODAY I'D LIKE TO RECEIVE AN INTUITIVE SIGN ABOUT:

_____
_____

GOALS TO HELP ME FEEL LESS SCATTERED AND MORE CENTERED TODAY:

_____   _____

_____   _____

HOW I PLAN TO CONNECT MINDFULLY WITH MY INTUITION TODAY:

_____
_____
_____

MY MORNING INTUITIVE ROUTINE INCLUDED:

☐ MEDITATION   ☐ TIME IN NATURE   ☐ SELF-CARE:_____

☐ PRAYER   ☐ A HEALTHY BREAKFAST   ☐ OTHER:_____

☐ JOURNALING   ☐ SACRED PAUSES   _____

GUT CHECK—WHAT IS THE STRONGEST INSTINCT I HAVE RIGHT NOW ABOUT
HOW TO APPROACH A SITUATION, PERSON, OR ISSUE I'M FACING TODAY?

_____
_____
_____

EVENING REFLECTION

HOW I'D RATE MY ABILITY TO CONNECT WITH MY INTUITION TODAY:

1	2	3	4	5	6	7	8	9	10

DISCONNECTED   CONNECTED

MEANINGFUL COINCIDENCES, THEMES, OR PATTERNS I ENCOUNTERED TODAY:

_____

_____

_____

INTUITIVE INSIGHTS I EXPERIENCED INTERNALLY OR PHYSICALLY:

_____

_____

THINGS THAT CONNECTED ME TO MY INTUITION TODAY:

☐ GETTING QUALITY QUIET TIME OR TIME ALONE

☐ MINDFULLY SLOWING DOWN

☐ LOWERING MY STRESS LEVELS

☐ HAVING NOURISHING WORK AND HOME ROUTINES

☐ KEEPING MY ENVIRONMENT TIDY AND INVITING

☐ LISTENING TO SOFT MUSIC OR NATURE SOUNDS

☐ PULLING AN ORACLE CARD FOR INSPIRATION

☐ OTHER:_____

WHERE/WHEN DID I FEEL MOST INTUITIVE TODAY?

_____

_____

WHAT WAS MOST ENCOURAGING, COMFORTING, OR EXCITING ABOUT
CONNECTING WITH MY INTUITION TODAY?

_____

_____

MORNING REFLECTION   DATE ___/___/___

HOW I'D RATE MY OPENNESS TO INTUITIVE GUIDANCE TODAY:

1   2   3   4   5   6   7   8   9   10

CLOSED/DISTRACTED   OPEN/GROUNDED

LAST NIGHT'S INTUITIVE DREAMS, OR INTUITIVE INSIGHTS WHEN I AWOKE:
_____
_____

TODAY I'D LIKE TO RECEIVE AN INTUITIVE SIGN ABOUT:
_____
_____

GOALS TO HELP ME FEEL LESS SCATTERED AND MORE CENTERED TODAY:
_____   _____
_____   _____

HOW I PLAN TO CONNECT MINDFULLY WITH MY INTUITION TODAY:
_____
_____
_____

MY MORNING INTUITIVE ROUTINE INCLUDED:

☐ MEDITATION   ☐ TIME IN NATURE   ☐ SELF-CARE:_____
☐ PRAYER   ☐ A HEALTHY BREAKFAST   ☐ OTHER:_____
☐ JOURNALING   ☐ SACRED PAUSES   _____

GUT CHECK—WHAT IS THE STRONGEST INSTINCT I HAVE RIGHT NOW ABOUT
HOW TO APPROACH A SITUATION, PERSON, OR ISSUE I'M FACING TODAY?
_____
_____

EVENING REFLECTION

HOW I'D RATE MY ABILITY TO CONNECT WITH MY INTUITION TODAY:

1   2   3   4   5   6   7   8   9   10

DISCONNECTED   CONNECTED

MEANINGFUL COINCIDENCES, THEMES, OR PATTERNS I ENCOUNTERED TODAY:

_____

_____

_____

INTUITIVE INSIGHTS I EXPERIENCED INTERNALLY OR PHYSICALLY:

_____

_____

THINGS THAT CONNECTED ME TO MY INTUITION TODAY:

☐ GETTING QUALITY QUIET TIME OR TIME ALONE

☐ MINDFULLY SLOWING DOWN

☐ LOWERING MY STRESS LEVELS

☐ HAVING NOURISHING WORK AND HOME ROUTINES

☐ KEEPING MY ENVIRONMENT TIDY AND INVITING

☐ LISTENING TO SOFT MUSIC OR NATURE SOUNDS

☐ PULLING AN ORACLE CARD FOR INSPIRATION

☐ OTHER:_____

WHERE/WHEN DID I FEEL MOST INTUITIVE TODAY?

_____

_____

WHAT WAS MOST ENCOURAGING, COMFORTING, OR EXCITING ABOUT
CONNECTING WITH MY INTUITION TODAY?

_____

_____

MORNING REFLECTION

DATE ___/___/___

HOW I'D RATE MY OPENNESS TO INTUITIVE GUIDANCE TODAY:

1   2   3   4   5   6   7   8   9   10

CLOSED/DISTRACTED   OPEN/GROUNDED

LAST NIGHT'S INTUITIVE DREAMS, OR INTUITIVE INSIGHTS WHEN I AWOKE:

_____

_____

TODAY I'D LIKE TO RECEIVE AN INTUITIVE SIGN ABOUT:

_____

_____

GOALS TO HELP ME FEEL LESS SCATTERED AND MORE CENTERED TODAY:

_____   _____

_____   _____

HOW I PLAN TO CONNECT MINDFULLY WITH MY INTUITION TODAY:

_____

_____

_____

MY MORNING INTUITIVE ROUTINE INCLUDED:

☐ MEDITATION   ☐ TIME IN NATURE   ☐ SELF-CARE:_____

☐ PRAYER   ☐ A HEALTHY BREAKFAST ☐ OTHER:_____

☐ JOURNALING   ☐ SACRED PAUSES   _____

GUT CHECK—WHAT IS THE STRONGEST INSTINCT I HAVE RIGHT NOW ABOUT
HOW TO APPROACH A SITUATION, PERSON, OR ISSUE I'M FACING TODAY?

_____

_____

_____

EVENING REFLECTION

HOW I'D RATE MY ABILITY TO CONNECT WITH MY INTUITION TODAY:

1	2	3	4	5	6	7	8	9	10

DISCONNECTED   CONNECTED

MEANINGFUL COINCIDENCES, THEMES, OR PATTERNS I ENCOUNTERED TODAY:

_____

_____

_____

INTUITIVE INSIGHTS I EXPERIENCED INTERNALLY OR PHYSICALLY:

_____

_____

THINGS THAT CONNECTED ME TO MY INTUITION TODAY:

☐ GETTING QUALITY QUIET TIME OR TIME ALONE

☐ MINDFULLY SLOWING DOWN

☐ LOWERING MY STRESS LEVELS

☐ HAVING NOURISHING WORK AND HOME ROUTINES

☐ KEEPING MY ENVIRONMENT TIDY AND INVITING

☐ LISTENING TO SOFT MUSIC OR NATURE SOUNDS

☐ PULLING AN ORACLE CARD FOR INSPIRATION

☐ OTHER:_____

WHERE/WHEN DID I FEEL MOST INTUITIVE TODAY?

_____

_____

WHAT WAS MOST ENCOURAGING, COMFORTING, OR EXCITING ABOUT
CONNECTING WITH MY INTUITION TODAY?

_____

_____

MORNING REFLECTION

DATE ___/___/___

HOW I'D RATE MY OPENNESS TO INTUITIVE GUIDANCE TODAY:

1   2   3   4   5   6   7   8   9   10

CLOSED/DISTRACTED   OPEN/GROUNDED

LAST NIGHT'S INTUITIVE DREAMS, OR INTUITIVE INSIGHTS WHEN I AWOKE:

_____

_____

TODAY I'D LIKE TO RECEIVE AN INTUITIVE SIGN ABOUT:

_____

_____

GOALS TO HELP ME FEEL LESS SCATTERED AND MORE CENTERED TODAY:

_____   _____

_____   _____

HOW I PLAN TO CONNECT MINDFULLY WITH MY INTUITION TODAY:

_____

_____

_____

MY MORNING INTUITIVE ROUTINE INCLUDED:

☐ MEDITATION   ☐ TIME IN NATURE   ☐ SELF-CARE:_____

☐ PRAYER   ☐ A HEALTHY BREAKFAST   ☐ OTHER:_____

☐ JOURNALING   ☐ SACRED PAUSES   _____

GUT CHECK—WHAT IS THE STRONGEST INSTINCT I HAVE RIGHT NOW ABOUT
HOW TO APPROACH A SITUATION, PERSON, OR ISSUE I'M FACING TODAY?

_____

_____

_____

EVENING REFLECTION

HOW I'D RATE MY ABILITY TO CONNECT WITH MY INTUITION TODAY:

1   2   3   4   5   6   7   8   9   10

DISCONNECTED   CONNECTED

MEANINGFUL COINCIDENCES, THEMES, OR PATTERNS I ENCOUNTERED TODAY:

_____

_____

_____

INTUITIVE INSIGHTS I EXPERIENCED INTERNALLY OR PHYSICALLY:

_____

_____

THINGS THAT CONNECTED ME TO MY INTUITION TODAY:

☐ GETTING QUALITY QUIET TIME OR TIME ALONE

☐ MINDFULLY SLOWING DOWN

☐ LOWERING MY STRESS LEVELS

☐ HAVING NOURISHING WORK AND HOME ROUTINES

☐ KEEPING MY ENVIRONMENT TIDY AND INVITING

☐ LISTENING TO SOFT MUSIC OR NATURE SOUNDS

☐ PULLING AN ORACLE CARD FOR INSPIRATION

☐ OTHER:_____

WHERE/WHEN DID I FEEL MOST INTUITIVE TODAY?

_____

_____

WHAT WAS MOST ENCOURAGING, COMFORTING, OR EXCITING ABOUT
CONNECTING WITH MY INTUITION TODAY?

_____

_____

MORNING REFLECTION   DATE ___/___/___

HOW I'D RATE MY OPENNESS TO INTUITIVE GUIDANCE TODAY:

1   2   3   4   5   6   7   8   9   10

CLOSED/DISTRACTED   OPEN/GROUNDED

LAST NIGHT'S INTUITIVE DREAMS, OR INTUITIVE INSIGHTS WHEN I AWOKE:

_____
_____

TODAY I'D LIKE TO RECEIVE AN INTUITIVE SIGN ABOUT:

_____
_____

GOALS TO HELP ME FEEL LESS SCATTERED AND MORE CENTERED TODAY:

_____   _____
_____   _____

HOW I PLAN TO CONNECT MINDFULLY WITH MY INTUITION TODAY:

_____
_____
_____

MY MORNING INTUITIVE ROUTINE INCLUDED:

☐ MEDITATION   ☐ TIME IN NATURE   ☐ SELF-CARE:_____

☐ PRAYER   ☐ A HEALTHY BREAKFAST   ☐ OTHER:_____

☐ JOURNALING   ☐ SACRED PAUSES   _____

GUT CHECK—WHAT IS THE STRONGEST INSTINCT I HAVE RIGHT NOW ABOUT
HOW TO APPROACH A SITUATION, PERSON, OR ISSUE I'M FACING TODAY?

_____
_____
_____

EVENING REFLECTION

HOW I'D RATE MY ABILITY TO CONNECT WITH MY INTUITION TODAY:

1   2   3   4   5   6   7   8   9   10

DISCONNECTED   CONNECTED

MEANINGFUL COINCIDENCES, THEMES, OR PATTERNS I ENCOUNTERED TODAY:
_____
_____
_____

INTUITIVE INSIGHTS I EXPERIENCED INTERNALLY OR PHYSICALLY:
_____
_____

THINGS THAT CONNECTED ME TO MY INTUITION TODAY:

☐ GETTING QUALITY QUIET TIME OR TIME ALONE

☐ MINDFULLY SLOWING DOWN

☐ LOWERING MY STRESS LEVELS

☐ HAVING NOURISHING WORK AND HOME ROUTINES

☐ KEEPING MY ENVIRONMENT TIDY AND INVITING

☐ LISTENING TO SOFT MUSIC OR NATURE SOUNDS

☐ PULLING AN ORACLE CARD FOR INSPIRATION

☐ OTHER:_____

WHERE/WHEN DID I FEEL MOST INTUITIVE TODAY?
_____
_____

WHAT WAS MOST ENCOURAGING, COMFORTING, OR EXCITING ABOUT
CONNECTING WITH MY INTUITION TODAY?
_____
_____

MORNING REFLECTION DATE ___/___/___

LAST NIGHT'S INTUITIVE DREAMS, OR INTUITIVE INSIGHTS WHEN I AWOKE:

_____

_____

TODAY I'D LIKE TO RECEIVE AN INTUITIVE SIGN ABOUT:

_____

_____

GOALS TO HELP ME FEEL LESS SCATTERED AND MORE CENTERED TODAY:

_____   _____

_____   _____

HOW I PLAN TO CONNECT MINDFULLY WITH MY INTUITION TODAY:

_____

_____

_____

MY MORNING INTUITIVE ROUTINE INCLUDED:

☐ MEDITATION   ☐ TIME IN NATURE   ☐ SELF-CARE:_____

☐ PRAYER   ☐ A HEALTHY BREAKFAST   ☐ OTHER:_____

☐ JOURNALING   ☐ SACRED PAUSES   _____

GUT CHECK—WHAT IS THE STRONGEST INSTINCT I HAVE RIGHT NOW ABOUT
HOW TO APPROACH A SITUATION, PERSON, OR ISSUE I'M FACING TODAY?

_____

_____

_____

EVENING REFLECTION

HOW I'D RATE MY ABILITY TO CONNECT WITH MY INTUITION TODAY:

1   2   3   4   5   6   7   8   9   10

DISCONNECTED   CONNECTED

MEANINGFUL COINCIDENCES, THEMES, OR PATTERNS I ENCOUNTERED TODAY:

_____

_____

_____

INTUITIVE INSIGHTS I EXPERIENCED INTERNALLY OR PHYSICALLY:

_____

_____

THINGS THAT CONNECTED ME TO MY INTUITION TODAY:

☐ GETTING QUALITY QUIET TIME OR TIME ALONE

☐ MINDFULLY SLOWING DOWN

☐ LOWERING MY STRESS LEVELS

☐ HAVING NOURISHING WORK AND HOME ROUTINES

☐ KEEPING MY ENVIRONMENT TIDY AND INVITING

☐ LISTENING TO SOFT MUSIC OR NATURE SOUNDS

☐ PULLING AN ORACLE CARD FOR INSPIRATION

☐ OTHER:_____

WHERE/WHEN DID I FEEL MOST INTUITIVE TODAY?

_____

_____

WHAT WAS MOST ENCOURAGING, COMFORTING, OR EXCITING ABOUT
CONNECTING WITH MY INTUITION TODAY?

_____

_____

MORNING REFLECTION DATE ___/___/___

HOW I'D RATE MY OPENNESS TO INTUITIVE GUIDANCE TODAY:

1   2   3   4   5   6   7   8   9   10

CLOSED/DISTRACTED   OPEN/GROUNDED

LAST NIGHT'S INTUITIVE DREAMS, OR INTUITIVE INSIGHTS WHEN I AWOKE:
_____
_____

TODAY I'D LIKE TO RECEIVE AN INTUITIVE SIGN ABOUT:
_____
_____

GOALS TO HELP ME FEEL LESS SCATTERED AND MORE CENTERED TODAY:
_____   _____
_____   _____

HOW I PLAN TO CONNECT MINDFULLY WITH MY INTUITION TODAY:
_____
_____
_____

MY MORNING INTUITIVE ROUTINE INCLUDED:

☐ MEDITATION   ☐ TIME IN NATURE   ☐ SELF-CARE:_____

☐ PRAYER   ☐ A HEALTHY BREAKFAST   ☐ OTHER:_____

☐ JOURNALING   ☐ SACRED PAUSES   _____

GUT CHECK—WHAT IS THE STRONGEST INSTINCT I HAVE RIGHT NOW ABOUT
HOW TO APPROACH A SITUATION, PERSON, OR ISSUE I'M FACING TODAY?
_____
_____

EVENING REFLECTION

HOW I'D RATE MY ABILITY TO CONNECT WITH MY INTUITION TODAY:

1   2   3   4   5   6   7   8   9   10

DISCONNECTED   CONNECTED

MEANINGFUL COINCIDENCES, THEMES, OR PATTERNS I ENCOUNTERED TODAY:

_____

_____

_____

INTUITIVE INSIGHTS I EXPERIENCED INTERNALLY OR PHYSICALLY:

_____

_____

THINGS THAT CONNECTED ME TO MY INTUITION TODAY:

☐ GETTING QUALITY QUIET TIME OR TIME ALONE

☐ MINDFULLY SLOWING DOWN

☐ LOWERING MY STRESS LEVELS

☐ HAVING NOURISHING WORK AND HOME ROUTINES

☐ KEEPING MY ENVIRONMENT TIDY AND INVITING

☐ LISTENING TO SOFT MUSIC OR NATURE SOUNDS

☐ PULLING AN ORACLE CARD FOR INSPIRATION

☐ OTHER:_____

WHERE/WHEN DID I FEEL MOST INTUITIVE TODAY?

_____

_____

WHAT WAS MOST ENCOURAGING, COMFORTING, OR EXCITING ABOUT
CONNECTING WITH MY INTUITION TODAY?

_____

_____

MORNING REFLECTION

HOW I'D RATE MY OPENNESS TO INTUITIVE GUIDANCE TODAY:

1   2   3   4   5   6   7   8   9   10

CLOSED/DISTRACTED   OPEN/GROUNDED

LAST NIGHT'S INTUITIVE DREAMS, OR INTUITIVE INSIGHTS WHEN I AWOKE:

_____

_____

TODAY I'D LIKE TO RECEIVE AN INTUITIVE SIGN ABOUT:

_____

_____

GOALS TO HELP ME FEEL LESS SCATTERED AND MORE CENTERED TODAY:

_____   _____

_____   _____

HOW I PLAN TO CONNECT MINDFULLY WITH MY INTUITION TODAY:

_____

_____

_____

MY MORNING INTUITIVE ROUTINE INCLUDED:

☐ MEDITATION   ☐ TIME IN NATURE   ☐ SELF-CARE:_____

☐ PRAYER   ·   ☐ A HEALTHY BREAKFAST   ☐ OTHER:_____

☐ JOURNALING   ☐ SACRED PAUSES   _____

GUT CHECK—WHAT IS THE STRONGEST INSTINCT I HAVE RIGHT NOW ABOUT
HOW TO APPROACH A SITUATION, PERSON, OR ISSUE I'M FACING TODAY?

_____

_____

_____

EVENING REFLECTION

HOW I'D RATE MY ABILITY TO CONNECT WITH MY INTUITION TODAY:

1   2   3   4   5   6   7   8   9   10

DISCONNECTED   CONNECTED

MEANINGFUL COINCIDENCES, THEMES, OR PATTERNS I ENCOUNTERED TODAY:

_____

_____

_____

INTUITIVE INSIGHTS I EXPERIENCED INTERNALLY OR PHYSICALLY:

_____

_____

THINGS THAT CONNECTED ME TO MY INTUITION TODAY:

☐ GETTING QUALITY QUIET TIME OR TIME ALONE

☐ MINDFULLY SLOWING DOWN

☐ LOWERING MY STRESS LEVELS

☐ HAVING NOURISHING WORK AND HOME ROUTINES

☐ KEEPING MY ENVIRONMENT TIDY AND INVITING

☐ LISTENING TO SOFT MUSIC OR NATURE SOUNDS

☐ PULLING AN ORACLE CARD FOR INSPIRATION

☐ OTHER:_____

WHERE/WHEN DID I FEEL MOST INTUITIVE TODAY?

_____

_____

WHAT WAS MOST ENCOURAGING, COMFORTING, OR EXCITING ABOUT
CONNECTING WITH MY INTUITION TODAY?

_____

_____

MORNING REFLECTION

DATE ___/___/___

HOW I'D RATE MY OPENNESS TO INTUITIVE GUIDANCE TODAY:

1   2   3   4   5   6   7   8   9   10

CLOSED/DISTRACTED   OPEN/GROUNDED

LAST NIGHT'S INTUITIVE DREAMS, OR INTUITIVE INSIGHTS WHEN I AWOKE:

_____

_____

TODAY I'D LIKE TO RECEIVE AN INTUITIVE SIGN ABOUT:

_____

_____

GOALS TO HELP ME FEEL LESS SCATTERED AND MORE CENTERED TODAY:

_____   _____

_____   _____

HOW I PLAN TO CONNECT MINDFULLY WITH MY INTUITION TODAY:

_____

_____

_____

MY MORNING INTUITIVE ROUTINE INCLUDED:

☐ MEDITATION   ☐ TIME IN NATURE   ☐ SELF-CARE:_____

☐ PRAYER   ☐ A HEALTHY BREAKFAST   ☐ OTHER:_____

☐ JOURNALING   ☐ SACRED PAUSES   _____

GUT CHECK—WHAT IS THE STRONGEST INSTINCT I HAVE RIGHT NOW ABOUT
HOW TO APPROACH A SITUATION, PERSON, OR ISSUE I'M FACING TODAY?

_____

_____

_____

EVENING REFLECTION

HOW I'D RATE MY ABILITY TO CONNECT WITH MY INTUITION TODAY:

1   2   3   4   5   6   7   8   9   10

DISCONNECTED   CONNECTED

MEANINGFUL COINCIDENCES, THEMES, OR PATTERNS I ENCOUNTERED TODAY:

_____
_____
_____

INTUITIVE INSIGHTS I EXPERIENCED INTERNALLY OR PHYSICALLY:

_____
_____

THINGS THAT CONNECTED ME TO MY INTUITION TODAY:

☐ GETTING QUALITY QUIET TIME OR TIME ALONE
☐ MINDFULLY SLOWING DOWN
☐ LOWERING MY STRESS LEVELS
☐ HAVING NOURISHING WORK AND HOME ROUTINES
☐ KEEPING MY ENVIRONMENT TIDY AND INVITING
☐ LISTENING TO SOFT MUSIC OR NATURE SOUNDS
☐ PULLING AN ORACLE CARD FOR INSPIRATION
☐ OTHER:_____

WHERE/WHEN DID I FEEL MOST INTUITIVE TODAY?

_____
_____

WHAT WAS MOST ENCOURAGING, COMFORTING, OR EXCITING ABOUT
CONNECTING WITH MY INTUITION TODAY?

_____
_____

MORNING REFLECTION   DATE ___/___/___

HOW I'D RATE MY OPENNESS TO INTUITIVE GUIDANCE TODAY:

1   2   3   4   5   6   7   8   9   10

CLOSED/DISTRACTED   OPEN/GROUNDED

LAST NIGHT'S INTUITIVE DREAMS, OR INTUITIVE INSIGHTS WHEN I AWOKE:
_____
_____

TODAY I'D LIKE TO RECEIVE AN INTUITIVE SIGN ABOUT:
_____
_____

GOALS TO HELP ME FEEL LESS SCATTERED AND MORE CENTERED TODAY:
_____   _____
_____   _____

HOW I PLAN TO CONNECT MINDFULLY WITH MY INTUITION TODAY:
_____
_____
_____

MY MORNING INTUITIVE ROUTINE INCLUDED:

☐ MEDITATION   ☐ TIME IN NATURE   ☐ SELF-CARE:_____
☐ PRAYER   ☐ A HEALTHY BREAKFAST   ☐ OTHER:_____
☐ JOURNALING   ☐ SACRED PAUSES   _____

GUT CHECK—WHAT IS THE STRONGEST INSTINCT I HAVE RIGHT NOW ABOUT
HOW TO APPROACH A SITUATION, PERSON, OR ISSUE I'M FACING TODAY?
_____
_____
_____

EVENING REFLECTION

HOW I'D RATE MY ABILITY TO CONNECT WITH MY INTUITION TODAY:

1   2   3   4   5   6   7   8   9   10

DISCONNECTED   CONNECTED

MEANINGFUL COINCIDENCES, THEMES, OR PATTERNS I ENCOUNTERED TODAY:

_____

_____

_____

INTUITIVE INSIGHTS I EXPERIENCED INTERNALLY OR PHYSICALLY:

_____

_____

THINGS THAT CONNECTED ME TO MY INTUITION TODAY:

☐ GETTING QUALITY QUIET TIME OR TIME ALONE

☐ MINDFULLY SLOWING DOWN

☐ LOWERING MY STRESS LEVELS

☐ HAVING NOURISHING WORK AND HOME ROUTINES

☐ KEEPING MY ENVIRONMENT TIDY AND INVITING

☐ LISTENING TO SOFT MUSIC OR NATURE SOUNDS

☐ PULLING AN ORACLE CARD FOR INSPIRATION

☐ OTHER:_____

WHERE/WHEN DID I FEEL MOST INTUITIVE TODAY?

_____

_____

WHAT WAS MOST ENCOURAGING, COMFORTING, OR EXCITING ABOUT CONNECTING WITH MY INTUITION TODAY?

_____

_____

MORNING REFLECTION

DATE ___/___/___

HOW I'D RATE MY OPENNESS TO INTUITIVE GUIDANCE TODAY:

1   2   3   4   5   6   7   8   9   10

CLOSED/DISTRACTED   OPEN/GROUNDED

LAST NIGHT'S INTUITIVE DREAMS, OR INTUITIVE INSIGHTS WHEN I AWOKE:
_____
_____

TODAY I'D LIKE TO RECEIVE AN INTUITIVE SIGN ABOUT:
_____
_____

GOALS TO HELP ME FEEL LESS SCATTERED AND MORE CENTERED TODAY:
_____   _____
_____   _____

HOW I PLAN TO CONNECT MINDFULLY WITH MY INTUITION TODAY:
_____
_____
_____

MY MORNING INTUITIVE ROUTINE INCLUDED:

☐ MEDITATION   ☐ TIME IN NATURE   ☐ SELF-CARE:_____
☐ PRAYER   ☐ A HEALTHY BREAKFAST   ☐ OTHER:_____
☐ JOURNALING   ☐ SACRED PAUSES   _____

GUT CHECK—WHAT IS THE STRONGEST INSTINCT I HAVE RIGHT NOW ABOUT
HOW TO APPROACH A SITUATION, PERSON, OR ISSUE I'M FACING TODAY?
_____
_____
_____

EVENING REFLECTION

HOW I'D RATE MY ABILITY TO CONNECT WITH MY INTUITION TODAY:

1   2   3   4   5   6   7   8   9   10

DISCONNECTED   CONNECTED

MEANINGFUL COINCIDENCES, THEMES, OR PATTERNS I ENCOUNTERED TODAY:

_____

_____

_____

INTUITIVE INSIGHTS I EXPERIENCED INTERNALLY OR PHYSICALLY:

_____

_____

THINGS THAT CONNECTED ME TO MY INTUITION TODAY:

- [ ] GETTING QUALITY QUIET TIME OR TIME ALONE
- [ ] MINDFULLY SLOWING DOWN
- [ ] LOWERING MY STRESS LEVELS
- [ ] HAVING NOURISHING WORK AND HOME ROUTINES
- [ ] KEEPING MY ENVIRONMENT TIDY AND INVITING
- [ ] LISTENING TO SOFT MUSIC OR NATURE SOUNDS
- [ ] PULLING AN ORACLE CARD FOR INSPIRATION
- [ ] OTHER:_____

WHERE/WHEN DID I FEEL MOST INTUITIVE TODAY?

_____

_____

WHAT WAS MOST ENCOURAGING, COMFORTING, OR EXCITING ABOUT CONNECTING WITH MY INTUITION TODAY?

_____

_____

MORNING REFLECTION   DATE ___/___/___

HOW I'D RATE MY OPENNESS TO INTUITIVE GUIDANCE TODAY:

1   2   3   4   5   6   7   8   9   10

CLOSED/DISTRACTED   OPEN/GROUNDED

LAST NIGHT'S INTUITIVE DREAMS, OR INTUITIVE INSIGHTS WHEN I AWOKE:
_____
_____

TODAY I'D LIKE TO RECEIVE AN INTUITIVE SIGN ABOUT:
_____
_____

GOALS TO HELP ME FEEL LESS SCATTERED AND MORE CENTERED TODAY:
_____   _____
_____   _____

HOW I PLAN TO CONNECT MINDFULLY WITH MY INTUITION TODAY:
_____
_____
_____

MY MORNING INTUITIVE ROUTINE INCLUDED:

☐ MEDITATION   ☐ TIME IN NATURE   ☐ SELF-CARE:_____

☐ PRAYER   ☐ A HEALTHY BREAKFAST   ☐ OTHER:_____

☐ JOURNALING   ☐ SACRED PAUSES   _____

GUT CHECK—WHAT IS THE STRONGEST INSTINCT I HAVE RIGHT NOW ABOUT
HOW TO APPROACH A SITUATION, PERSON, OR ISSUE I'M FACING TODAY?
_____
_____
_____

EVENING REFLECTION

HOW I'D RATE MY ABILITY TO CONNECT WITH MY INTUITION TODAY:

1   2   3   4   5   6   7   8   9   10

DISCONNECTED   CONNECTED

MEANINGFUL COINCIDENCES, THEMES, OR PATTERNS I ENCOUNTERED TODAY:
_____
_____
_____

INTUITIVE INSIGHTS I EXPERIENCED INTERNALLY OR PHYSICALLY:
_____
_____

THINGS THAT CONNECTED ME TO MY INTUITION TODAY:

- ☐ GETTING QUALITY QUIET TIME OR TIME ALONE
- ☐ MINDFULLY SLOWING DOWN
- ☐ LOWERING MY STRESS LEVELS
- ☐ HAVING NOURISHING WORK AND HOME ROUTINES
- ☐ KEEPING MY ENVIRONMENT TIDY AND INVITING
- ☐ LISTENING TO SOFT MUSIC OR NATURE SOUNDS
- ☐ PULLING AN ORACLE CARD FOR INSPIRATION
- ☐ OTHER:_____

WHERE/WHEN DID I FEEL MOST INTUITIVE TODAY?
_____
_____

WHAT WAS MOST ENCOURAGING, COMFORTING, OR EXCITING ABOUT
CONNECTING WITH MY INTUITION TODAY?
_____
_____

MORNING REFLECTION

DATE ___ / ___ / ___

HOW I'D RATE MY OPENNESS TO INTUITIVE GUIDANCE TODAY:

1   2   3   4   5   6   7   8   9   10

CLOSED/DISTRACTED   OPEN/GROUNDED

LAST NIGHT'S INTUITIVE DREAMS, OR INTUITIVE INSIGHTS WHEN I AWOKE:
_____
_____

TODAY I'D LIKE TO RECEIVE AN INTUITIVE SIGN ABOUT:
_____
_____

GOALS TO HELP ME FEEL LESS SCATTERED AND MORE CENTERED TODAY:
_____   _____
_____   _____

HOW I PLAN TO CONNECT MINDFULLY WITH MY INTUITION TODAY:
_____
_____
_____

MY MORNING INTUITIVE ROUTINE INCLUDED:

☐ MEDITATION   ☐ TIME IN NATURE   ☐ SELF-CARE:_____
☐ PRAYER   ☐ A HEALTHY BREAKFAST   ☐ OTHER:_____
☐ JOURNALING   ☐ SACRED PAUSES   _____

GUT CHECK—WHAT IS THE STRONGEST INSTINCT I HAVE RIGHT NOW ABOUT
HOW TO APPROACH A SITUATION, PERSON, OR ISSUE I'M FACING TODAY?
_____
_____

EVENING REFLECTION

HOW I'D RATE MY ABILITY TO CONNECT WITH MY INTUITION TODAY:

1	2	3	4	5	6	7	8	9	10

DISCONNECTED   CONNECTED

MEANINGFUL COINCIDENCES, THEMES, OR PATTERNS I ENCOUNTERED TODAY:

_____

_____

_____

INTUITIVE INSIGHTS I EXPERIENCED INTERNALLY OR PHYSICALLY:

_____

_____

THINGS THAT CONNECTED ME TO MY INTUITION TODAY:

☐ GETTING QUALITY QUIET TIME OR TIME ALONE

☐ MINDFULLY SLOWING DOWN

☐ LOWERING MY STRESS LEVELS

☐ HAVING NOURISHING WORK AND HOME ROUTINES

☐ KEEPING MY ENVIRONMENT TIDY AND INVITING

☐ LISTENING TO SOFT MUSIC OR NATURE SOUNDS

☐ PULLING AN ORACLE CARD FOR INSPIRATION

☐ OTHER:_____

WHERE/WHEN DID I FEEL MOST INTUITIVE TODAY?

_____

_____

WHAT WAS MOST ENCOURAGING, COMFORTING, OR EXCITING ABOUT
CONNECTING WITH MY INTUITION TODAY?

_____

_____

MORNING REFLECTION

DATE ___/___/___

HOW I'D RATE MY OPENNESS TO INTUITIVE GUIDANCE TODAY:

1   2   3   4   5   6   7   8   9   10

CLOSED/DISTRACTED   OPEN/GROUNDED

LAST NIGHT'S INTUITIVE DREAMS, OR INTUITIVE INSIGHTS WHEN I AWOKE:

_____

_____

TODAY I'D LIKE TO RECEIVE AN INTUITIVE SIGN ABOUT:

_____

_____

GOALS TO HELP ME FEEL LESS SCATTERED AND MORE CENTERED TODAY:

_____   _____

_____   _____

HOW I PLAN TO CONNECT MINDFULLY WITH MY INTUITION TODAY:

_____

_____

_____

MY MORNING INTUITIVE ROUTINE INCLUDED:

☐ MEDITATION   ☐ TIME IN NATURE   ☐ SELF-CARE:_____

☐ PRAYER   ☐ A HEALTHY BREAKFAST   ☐ OTHER:_____

☐ JOURNALING   ☐ SACRED PAUSES   _____

GUT CHECK—WHAT IS THE STRONGEST INSTINCT I HAVE RIGHT NOW ABOUT
HOW TO APPROACH A SITUATION, PERSON, OR ISSUE I'M FACING TODAY?

_____

_____

_____

EVENING REFLECTION

HOW I'D RATE MY ABILITY TO CONNECT WITH MY INTUITION TODAY:

1   2   3   4   5   6   7   8   9   10

DISCONNECTED   CONNECTED

MEANINGFUL COINCIDENCES, THEMES, OR PATTERNS I ENCOUNTERED TODAY:

_____

_____

_____

INTUITIVE INSIGHTS I EXPERIENCED INTERNALLY OR PHYSICALLY:

_____

_____

THINGS THAT CONNECTED ME TO MY INTUITION TODAY:

☐ GETTING QUALITY QUIET TIME OR TIME ALONE

☐ MINDFULLY SLOWING DOWN

☐ LOWERING MY STRESS LEVELS

☐ HAVING NOURISHING WORK AND HOME ROUTINES

☐ KEEPING MY ENVIRONMENT TIDY AND INVITING

☐ LISTENING TO SOFT MUSIC OR NATURE SOUNDS

☐ PULLING AN ORACLE CARD FOR INSPIRATION

☐ OTHER:_____

WHERE/WHEN DID I FEEL MOST INTUITIVE TODAY?

_____

_____

WHAT WAS MOST ENCOURAGING, COMFORTING, OR EXCITING ABOUT
CONNECTING WITH MY INTUITION TODAY?

_____

_____

MORNING REFLECTION

DATE ___/___/___

LAST NIGHT'S INTUITIVE DREAMS, OR INTUITIVE INSIGHTS WHEN I AWOKE:

_____

_____

TODAY I'D LIKE TO RECEIVE AN INTUITIVE SIGN ABOUT:

_____

_____

GOALS TO HELP ME FEEL LESS SCATTERED AND MORE CENTERED TODAY:

_____   _____

_____   _____

HOW I PLAN TO CONNECT MINDFULLY WITH MY INTUITION TODAY:

_____

_____

_____

MY MORNING INTUITIVE ROUTINE INCLUDED:

☐ MEDITATION   ☐ TIME IN NATURE   ☐ SELF-CARE:_____

☐ PRAYER   ☐ A HEALTHY BREAKFAST   ☐ OTHER:_____

☐ JOURNALING   ☐ SACRED PAUSES   _____

GUT CHECK—WHAT IS THE STRONGEST INSTINCT I HAVE RIGHT NOW ABOUT
HOW TO APPROACH A SITUATION, PERSON, OR ISSUE I'M FACING TODAY?

_____

_____

_____

EVENING REFLECTION

HOW I'D RATE MY ABILITY TO CONNECT WITH MY INTUITION TODAY:

1   2   3   4   5   6   7   8   9   10

DISCONNECTED   CONNECTED

MEANINGFUL COINCIDENCES, THEMES, OR PATTERNS I ENCOUNTERED TODAY:

_____

_____

_____

INTUITIVE INSIGHTS I EXPERIENCED INTERNALLY OR PHYSICALLY:

_____

_____

THINGS THAT CONNECTED ME TO MY INTUITION TODAY:

- [ ] GETTING QUALITY QUIET TIME OR TIME ALONE
- [ ] MINDFULLY SLOWING DOWN
- [ ] LOWERING MY STRESS LEVELS
- [ ] HAVING NOURISHING WORK AND HOME ROUTINES
- [ ] KEEPING MY ENVIRONMENT TIDY AND INVITING
- [ ] LISTENING TO SOFT MUSIC OR NATURE SOUNDS
- [ ] PULLING AN ORACLE CARD FOR INSPIRATION
- [ ] OTHER:_____

WHERE/WHEN DID I FEEL MOST INTUITIVE TODAY?

_____

_____

WHAT WAS MOST ENCOURAGING, COMFORTING, OR EXCITING ABOUT CONNECTING WITH MY INTUITION TODAY?

_____

_____

MORNING REFLECTION   DATE ___/___/___

HOW I'D RATE MY OPENNESS TO INTUITIVE GUIDANCE TODAY:

1   2   3   4   5   6   7   8   9   10

CLOSED/DISTRACTED   OPEN/GROUNDED

LAST NIGHT'S INTUITIVE DREAMS, OR INTUITIVE INSIGHTS WHEN I AWOKE:

_____

_____

TODAY I'D LIKE TO RECEIVE AN INTUITIVE SIGN ABOUT:

_____

_____

GOALS TO HELP ME FEEL LESS SCATTERED AND MORE CENTERED TODAY:

_____   _____

_____   _____

HOW I PLAN TO CONNECT MINDFULLY WITH MY INTUITION TODAY:

_____

_____

_____

MY MORNING INTUITIVE ROUTINE INCLUDED:

☐ MEDITATION   ☐ TIME IN NATURE   ☐ SELF-CARE:_____

☐ PRAYER   ☐ A HEALTHY BREAKFAST   ☐ OTHER:_____

☐ JOURNALING   ☐ SACRED PAUSES   _____

GUT CHECK—WHAT IS THE STRONGEST INSTINCT I HAVE RIGHT NOW ABOUT
HOW TO APPROACH A SITUATION, PERSON, OR ISSUE I'M FACING TODAY?

_____

_____

_____

EVENING REFLECTION

HOW I'D RATE MY ABILITY TO CONNECT WITH MY INTUITION TODAY:

| 1 | 2 | 3 | 4 | 5 | 6 | 7 | 8 | 9 | 10 |

DISCONNECTED   CONNECTED

MEANINGFUL COINCIDENCES, THEMES, OR PATTERNS I ENCOUNTERED TODAY:

_____

_____

_____

INTUITIVE INSIGHTS I EXPERIENCED INTERNALLY OR PHYSICALLY:

_____

_____

THINGS THAT CONNECTED ME TO MY INTUITION TODAY:

☐ GETTING QUALITY QUIET TIME OR TIME ALONE

☐ MINDFULLY SLOWING DOWN

☐ LOWERING MY STRESS LEVELS

☐ HAVING NOURISHING WORK AND HOME ROUTINES

☐ KEEPING MY ENVIRONMENT TIDY AND INVITING

☐ LISTENING TO SOFT MUSIC OR NATURE SOUNDS

☐ PULLING AN ORACLE CARD FOR INSPIRATION

☐ OTHER:_____

WHERE/WHEN DID I FEEL MOST INTUITIVE TODAY?

_____

_____

WHAT WAS MOST ENCOURAGING, COMFORTING, OR EXCITING ABOUT
CONNECTING WITH MY INTUITION TODAY?

_____

_____

MORNING REFLECTION

DATE ___/___/___

HOW I'D RATE MY OPENNESS TO INTUITIVE GUIDANCE TODAY:

1   2   3   4   5   6   7   8   9   10

CLOSED/DISTRACTED   OPEN/GROUNDED

LAST NIGHT'S INTUITIVE DREAMS, OR INTUITIVE INSIGHTS WHEN I AWOKE:

_____

_____

TODAY I'D LIKE TO RECEIVE AN INTUITIVE SIGN ABOUT:

_____

_____

GOALS TO HELP ME FEEL LESS SCATTERED AND MORE CENTERED TODAY:

_____   _____

_____   _____

HOW I PLAN TO CONNECT MINDFULLY WITH MY INTUITION TODAY:

_____

_____

_____

MY MORNING INTUITIVE ROUTINE INCLUDED:

☐ MEDITATION   ☐ TIME IN NATURE   ☐ SELF-CARE:_____

☐ PRAYER   ☐ A HEALTHY BREAKFAST   ☐ OTHER:_____

☐ JOURNALING   ☐ SACRED PAUSES   _____

GUT CHECK—WHAT IS THE STRONGEST INSTINCT I HAVE RIGHT NOW ABOUT
HOW TO APPROACH A SITUATION, PERSON, OR ISSUE I'M FACING TODAY?

_____

_____

_____

EVENING REFLECTION

HOW I'D RATE MY ABILITY TO CONNECT WITH MY INTUITION TODAY:

1   2   3   4   5   6   7   8   9   10

DISCONNECTED   CONNECTED

MEANINGFUL COINCIDENCES, THEMES, OR PATTERNS I ENCOUNTERED TODAY:

_____

_____

_____

INTUITIVE INSIGHTS I EXPERIENCED INTERNALLY OR PHYSICALLY:

_____

_____

THINGS THAT CONNECTED ME TO MY INTUITION TODAY:

☐ GETTING QUALITY QUIET TIME OR TIME ALONE

☐ MINDFULLY SLOWING DOWN

☐ LOWERING MY STRESS LEVELS

☐ HAVING NOURISHING WORK AND HOME ROUTINES

☐ KEEPING MY ENVIRONMENT TIDY AND INVITING

☐ LISTENING TO SOFT MUSIC OR NATURE SOUNDS

☐ PULLING AN ORACLE CARD FOR INSPIRATION

☐ OTHER:_____

WHERE/WHEN DID I FEEL MOST INTUITIVE TODAY?

_____

_____

WHAT WAS MOST ENCOURAGING, COMFORTING, OR EXCITING ABOUT
CONNECTING WITH MY INTUITION TODAY?

_____

_____

MORNING REFLECTION DATE ___/___/___

HOW I'D RATE MY OPENNESS TO INTUITIVE GUIDANCE TODAY:

1   2   3   4   5   6   7   8   9   10

CLOSED/DISTRACTED   OPEN/GROUNDED

LAST NIGHT'S INTUITIVE DREAMS, OR INTUITIVE INSIGHTS WHEN I AWOKE:

_____

_____

TODAY I'D LIKE TO RECEIVE AN INTUITIVE SIGN ABOUT:

_____

_____

GOALS TO HELP ME FEEL LESS SCATTERED AND MORE CENTERED TODAY:

_____   _____

_____   _____

HOW I PLAN TO CONNECT MINDFULLY WITH MY INTUITION TODAY:

_____

_____

_____

MY MORNING INTUITIVE ROUTINE INCLUDED:

☐ MEDITATION   ☐ TIME IN NATURE   ☐ SELF-CARE:_____

☐ PRAYER   ☐ A HEALTHY BREAKFAST   ☐ OTHER:_____

☐ JOURNALING   ☐ SACRED PAUSES   _____

GUT CHECK—WHAT IS THE STRONGEST INSTINCT I HAVE RIGHT NOW ABOUT HOW TO APPROACH A SITUATION, PERSON, OR ISSUE I'M FACING TODAY?

_____

_____

_____

EVENING REFLECTION

HOW I'D RATE MY ABILITY TO CONNECT WITH MY INTUITION TODAY:

1   2   3   4   5   6   7   8   9   10

DISCONNECTED   CONNECTED

MEANINGFUL COINCIDENCES, THEMES, OR PATTERNS I ENCOUNTERED TODAY:

_____

_____

_____

INTUITIVE INSIGHTS I EXPERIENCED INTERNALLY OR PHYSICALLY:

_____

_____

THINGS THAT CONNECTED ME TO MY INTUITION TODAY:

- [ ] GETTING QUALITY QUIET TIME OR TIME ALONE
- [ ] MINDFULLY SLOWING DOWN
- [ ] LOWERING MY STRESS LEVELS
- [ ] HAVING NOURISHING WORK AND HOME ROUTINES
- [ ] KEEPING MY ENVIRONMENT TIDY AND INVITING
- [ ] LISTENING TO SOFT MUSIC OR NATURE SOUNDS
- [ ] PULLING AN ORACLE CARD FOR INSPIRATION
- [ ] OTHER:_____

WHERE/WHEN DID I FEEL MOST INTUITIVE TODAY?

_____

_____

WHAT WAS MOST ENCOURAGING, COMFORTING, OR EXCITING ABOUT
CONNECTING WITH MY INTUITION TODAY?

_____

_____

MORNING REFLECTION DATE ___/___/___

LAST NIGHT'S INTUITIVE DREAMS, OR INTUITIVE INSIGHTS WHEN I AWOKE:

_____

_____

TODAY I'D LIKE TO RECEIVE AN INTUITIVE SIGN ABOUT:

_____

_____

GOALS TO HELP ME FEEL LESS SCATTERED AND MORE CENTERED TODAY:

_____   _____

_____   _____

HOW I PLAN TO CONNECT MINDFULLY WITH MY INTUITION TODAY:

_____

_____

_____

MY MORNING INTUITIVE ROUTINE INCLUDED:

☐ MEDITATION   ☐ TIME IN NATURE   ☐ SELF-CARE:_____

☐ PRAYER   ☐ A HEALTHY BREAKFAST   ☐ OTHER:_____

☐ JOURNALING   ☐ SACRED PAUSES   _____

GUT CHECK—WHAT IS THE STRONGEST INSTINCT I HAVE RIGHT NOW ABOUT
HOW TO APPROACH A SITUATION, PERSON, OR ISSUE I'M FACING TODAY?

_____

_____

EVENING REFLECTION

HOW I'D RATE MY ABILITY TO CONNECT WITH MY INTUITION TODAY:

1   2   3   4   5   6   7   8   9   10

DISCONNECTED   CONNECTED

MEANINGFUL COINCIDENCES, THEMES, OR PATTERNS I ENCOUNTERED TODAY:

_____

_____

_____

INTUITIVE INSIGHTS I EXPERIENCED INTERNALLY OR PHYSICALLY:

_____

_____

THINGS THAT CONNECTED ME TO MY INTUITION TODAY:

☐ GETTING QUALITY QUIET TIME OR TIME ALONE

☐ MINDFULLY SLOWING DOWN

☐ LOWERING MY STRESS LEVELS

☐ HAVING NOURISHING WORK AND HOME ROUTINES

☐ KEEPING MY ENVIRONMENT TIDY AND INVITING

☐ LISTENING TO SOFT MUSIC OR NATURE SOUNDS

☐ PULLING AN ORACLE CARD FOR INSPIRATION

☐ OTHER:_____

WHERE/WHEN DID I FEEL MOST INTUITIVE TODAY?

_____

_____

WHAT WAS MOST ENCOURAGING, COMFORTING, OR EXCITING ABOUT
CONNECTING WITH MY INTUITION TODAY?

_____

_____

MORNING REFLECTION

DATE ___/___/___

LAST NIGHT'S INTUITIVE DREAMS, OR INTUITIVE INSIGHTS WHEN I AWOKE:

_____

_____

TODAY I'D LIKE TO RECEIVE AN INTUITIVE SIGN ABOUT:

_____

_____

GOALS TO HELP ME FEEL LESS SCATTERED AND MORE CENTERED TODAY:

_____   _____

_____   _____

HOW I PLAN TO CONNECT MINDFULLY WITH MY INTUITION TODAY:

_____

_____

_____

MY MORNING INTUITIVE ROUTINE INCLUDED:

☐ MEDITATION   ☐ TIME IN NATURE   ☐ SELF-CARE:_____

☐ PRAYER   ☐ A HEALTHY BREAKFAST   ☐ OTHER:_____

☐ JOURNALING   ☐ SACRED PAUSES   _____

GUT CHECK—WHAT IS THE STRONGEST INSTINCT I HAVE RIGHT NOW ABOUT
HOW TO APPROACH A SITUATION, PERSON, OR ISSUE I'M FACING TODAY?

_____

_____

_____

EVENING REFLECTION

HOW I'D RATE MY ABILITY TO CONNECT WITH MY INTUITION TODAY:

1	2	3	4	5	6	7	8	9	10

DISCONNECTED   CONNECTED

MEANINGFUL COINCIDENCES, THEMES, OR PATTERNS I ENCOUNTERED TODAY:

_____

_____

_____

INTUITIVE INSIGHTS I EXPERIENCED INTERNALLY OR PHYSICALLY:

_____

_____

THINGS THAT CONNECTED ME TO MY INTUITION TODAY:

☐ GETTING QUALITY QUIET TIME OR TIME ALONE

☐ MINDFULLY SLOWING DOWN

☐ LOWERING MY STRESS LEVELS

☐ HAVING NOURISHING WORK AND HOME ROUTINES

☐ KEEPING MY ENVIRONMENT TIDY AND INVITING

☐ LISTENING TO SOFT MUSIC OR NATURE SOUNDS

☐ PULLING AN ORACLE CARD FOR INSPIRATION

☐ OTHER:_____

WHERE/WHEN DID I FEEL MOST INTUITIVE TODAY?

_____

_____

WHAT WAS MOST ENCOURAGING, COMFORTING, OR EXCITING ABOUT CONNECTING WITH MY INTUITION TODAY?

_____

_____

MORNING REFLECTION DATE ___/___/___

LAST NIGHT'S INTUITIVE DREAMS, OR INTUITIVE INSIGHTS WHEN I AWOKE:

_____

_____

TODAY I'D LIKE TO RECEIVE AN INTUITIVE SIGN ABOUT:

_____

_____

GOALS TO HELP ME FEEL LESS SCATTERED AND MORE CENTERED TODAY:

_____   _____

_____   _____

HOW I PLAN TO CONNECT MINDFULLY WITH MY INTUITION TODAY:

_____

_____

_____

MY MORNING INTUITIVE ROUTINE INCLUDED:

☐ MEDITATION   ☐ TIME IN NATURE   ☐ SELF-CARE:_____

☐ PRAYER   ☐ A HEALTHY BREAKFAST   ☐ OTHER:_____

☐ JOURNALING   ☐ SACRED PAUSES   _____

GUT CHECK—WHAT IS THE STRONGEST INSTINCT I HAVE RIGHT NOW ABOUT
HOW TO APPROACH A SITUATION, PERSON, OR ISSUE I'M FACING TODAY?

_____

_____

_____

EVENING REFLECTION

HOW I'D RATE MY ABILITY TO CONNECT WITH MY INTUITION TODAY:

1	2	3	4	5	6	7	8	9	10

DISCONNECTED   CONNECTED

MEANINGFUL COINCIDENCES, THEMES, OR PATTERNS I ENCOUNTERED TODAY:

_____

_____

_____

INTUITIVE INSIGHTS I EXPERIENCED INTERNALLY OR PHYSICALLY:

_____

_____

THINGS THAT CONNECTED ME TO MY INTUITION TODAY:

- [ ] GETTING QUALITY QUIET TIME OR TIME ALONE
- [ ] MINDFULLY SLOWING DOWN
- [ ] LOWERING MY STRESS LEVELS
- [ ] HAVING NOURISHING WORK AND HOME ROUTINES
- [ ] KEEPING MY ENVIRONMENT TIDY AND INVITING
- [ ] LISTENING TO SOFT MUSIC OR NATURE SOUNDS
- [ ] PULLING AN ORACLE CARD FOR INSPIRATION
- [ ] OTHER:_____

WHERE/WHEN DID I FEEL MOST INTUITIVE TODAY?

_____

_____

WHAT WAS MOST ENCOURAGING, COMFORTING, OR EXCITING ABOUT
CONNECTING WITH MY INTUITION TODAY?

_____

_____

MORNING REFLECTION   DATE ___ / ___ / ___

HOW I'D RATE MY OPENNESS TO INTUITIVE GUIDANCE TODAY:

1   2   3   4   5   6   7   8   9   10

CLOSED/DISTRACTED   OPEN/GROUNDED

LAST NIGHT'S INTUITIVE DREAMS, OR INTUITIVE INSIGHTS WHEN I AWOKE:

_____

_____

TODAY I'D LIKE TO RECEIVE AN INTUITIVE SIGN ABOUT:

_____

_____

GOALS TO HELP ME FEEL LESS SCATTERED AND MORE CENTERED TODAY:

_____   _____

_____   _____

HOW I PLAN TO CONNECT MINDFULLY WITH MY INTUITION TODAY:

_____

_____

_____

MY MORNING INTUITIVE ROUTINE INCLUDED:

☐ MEDITATION   ☐ TIME IN NATURE   ☐ SELF-CARE:_____

☐ PRAYER   ☐ A HEALTHY BREAKFAST   ☐ OTHER:_____

☐ JOURNALING   ☐ SACRED PAUSES   _____

GUT CHECK—WHAT IS THE STRONGEST INSTINCT I HAVE RIGHT NOW ABOUT
HOW TO APPROACH A SITUATION, PERSON, OR ISSUE I'M FACING TODAY?

_____

_____

_____

EVENING REFLECTION

HOW I'D RATE MY ABILITY TO CONNECT WITH MY INTUITION TODAY:

1   2   3   4   5   6   7   8   9   10

DISCONNECTED   CONNECTED

MEANINGFUL COINCIDENCES, THEMES, OR PATTERNS I ENCOUNTERED TODAY:

_____

_____

_____

INTUITIVE INSIGHTS I EXPERIENCED INTERNALLY OR PHYSICALLY:

_____

_____

THINGS THAT CONNECTED ME TO MY INTUITION TODAY:

- ☐ GETTING QUALITY QUIET TIME OR TIME ALONE
- ☐ MINDFULLY SLOWING DOWN
- ☐ LOWERING MY STRESS LEVELS
- ☐ HAVING NOURISHING WORK AND HOME ROUTINES
- ☐ KEEPING MY ENVIRONMENT TIDY AND INVITING
- ☐ LISTENING TO SOFT MUSIC OR NATURE SOUNDS
- ☐ PULLING AN ORACLE CARD FOR INSPIRATION
- ☐ OTHER:_____

WHERE/WHEN DID I FEEL MOST INTUITIVE TODAY?

_____

_____

WHAT WAS MOST ENCOURAGING, COMFORTING, OR EXCITING ABOUT
CONNECTING WITH MY INTUITION TODAY?

_____

_____

MORNING REFLECTION

DATE ___/___/___

HOW I'D RATE MY OPENNESS TO INTUITIVE GUIDANCE TODAY:

1   2   3   4   5   6   7   8   9   10

CLOSED/DISTRACTED   OPEN/GROUNDED

LAST NIGHT'S INTUITIVE DREAMS, OR INTUITIVE INSIGHTS WHEN I AWOKE:

_____

_____

TODAY I'D LIKE TO RECEIVE AN INTUITIVE SIGN ABOUT:

_____

_____

GOALS TO HELP ME FEEL LESS SCATTERED AND MORE CENTERED TODAY:

_____   _____

_____   _____

HOW I PLAN TO CONNECT MINDFULLY WITH MY INTUITION TODAY:

_____

_____

_____

MY MORNING INTUITIVE ROUTINE INCLUDED:

☐ MEDITATION   ☐ TIME IN NATURE   ☐ SELF-CARE:_____

☐ PRAYER   ☐ A HEALTHY BREAKFAST   ☐ OTHER:_____

☐ JOURNALING   ☐ SACRED PAUSES   _____

GUT CHECK—WHAT IS THE STRONGEST INSTINCT I HAVE RIGHT NOW ABOUT
HOW TO APPROACH A SITUATION, PERSON, OR ISSUE I'M FACING TODAY?

_____

_____

_____

EVENING REFLECTION

MEANINGFUL COINCIDENCES, THEMES, OR PATTERNS I ENCOUNTERED TODAY:

_____

_____

_____

INTUITIVE INSIGHTS I EXPERIENCED INTERNALLY OR PHYSICALLY:

_____

_____

THINGS THAT CONNECTED ME TO MY INTUITION TODAY:

☐ GETTING QUALITY QUIET TIME OR TIME ALONE

☐ MINDFULLY SLOWING DOWN

☐ LOWERING MY STRESS LEVELS

☐ HAVING NOURISHING WORK AND HOME ROUTINES

☐ KEEPING MY ENVIRONMENT TIDY AND INVITING

☐ LISTENING TO SOFT MUSIC OR NATURE SOUNDS

☐ PULLING AN ORACLE CARD FOR INSPIRATION

☐ OTHER:_____

WHERE/WHEN DID I FEEL MOST INTUITIVE TODAY?

_____

_____

WHAT WAS MOST ENCOURAGING, COMFORTING, OR EXCITING ABOUT
CONNECTING WITH MY INTUITION TODAY?

_____

_____

MORNING REFLECTION   DATE ___/___/___

LAST NIGHT'S INTUITIVE DREAMS, OR INTUITIVE INSIGHTS WHEN I AWOKE:

_____

_____

TODAY I'D LIKE TO RECEIVE AN INTUITIVE SIGN ABOUT:

_____

_____

GOALS TO HELP ME FEEL LESS SCATTERED AND MORE CENTERED TODAY:

_____   _____

_____   _____

HOW I PLAN TO CONNECT MINDFULLY WITH MY INTUITION TODAY:

_____

_____

_____

MY MORNING INTUITIVE ROUTINE INCLUDED:

☐ MEDITATION   ☐ TIME IN NATURE   ☐ SELF-CARE:_____

☐ PRAYER   ☐ A HEALTHY BREAKFAST   ☐ OTHER:_____

☐ JOURNALING   ☐ SACRED PAUSES   _____

GUT CHECK—WHAT IS THE STRONGEST INSTINCT I HAVE RIGHT NOW ABOUT
HOW TO APPROACH A SITUATION, PERSON, OR ISSUE I'M FACING TODAY?

_____

_____

_____

EVENING REFLECTION

HOW I'D RATE MY ABILITY TO CONNECT WITH MY INTUITION TODAY:

1   2   3   4   5   6   7   8   9   10

DISCONNECTED   CONNECTED

MEANINGFUL COINCIDENCES, THEMES, OR PATTERNS I ENCOUNTERED TODAY:

_____

_____

_____

INTUITIVE INSIGHTS I EXPERIENCED INTERNALLY OR PHYSICALLY:

_____

_____

THINGS THAT CONNECTED ME TO MY INTUITION TODAY:

☐ GETTING QUALITY QUIET TIME OR TIME ALONE

☐ MINDFULLY SLOWING DOWN

☐ LOWERING MY STRESS LEVELS

☐ HAVING NOURISHING WORK AND HOME ROUTINES

☐ KEEPING MY ENVIRONMENT TIDY AND INVITING

☐ LISTENING TO SOFT MUSIC OR NATURE SOUNDS

☐ PULLING AN ORACLE CARD FOR INSPIRATION

☐ OTHER:_____

WHERE/WHEN DID I FEEL MOST INTUITIVE TODAY?

_____

_____

WHAT WAS MOST ENCOURAGING, COMFORTING, OR EXCITING ABOUT
CONNECTING WITH MY INTUITION TODAY?

_____

_____

MORNING REFLECTION DATE ___/___/___

HOW I'D RATE MY OPENNESS TO INTUITIVE GUIDANCE TODAY:

1   2   3   4   5   6   7   8   9   10

CLOSED/DISTRACTED   OPEN/GROUNDED

LAST NIGHT'S INTUITIVE DREAMS, OR INTUITIVE INSIGHTS WHEN I AWOKE:

_____

_____

TODAY I'D LIKE TO RECEIVE AN INTUITIVE SIGN ABOUT:

_____

_____

GOALS TO HELP ME FEEL LESS SCATTERED AND MORE CENTERED TODAY:

_____   _____

_____   _____

HOW I PLAN TO CONNECT MINDFULLY WITH MY INTUITION TODAY:

_____

_____

_____

MY MORNING INTUITIVE ROUTINE INCLUDED:

☐ MEDITATION   ☐ TIME IN NATURE   ☐ SELF-CARE:_____

☐ PRAYER   ☐ A HEALTHY BREAKFAST   ☐ OTHER:_____

☐ JOURNALING   ☐ SACRED PAUSES   _____

GUT CHECK—WHAT IS THE STRONGEST INSTINCT I HAVE RIGHT NOW ABOUT
HOW TO APPROACH A SITUATION, PERSON, OR ISSUE I'M FACING TODAY?

_____

_____

_____

EVENING REFLECTION

1   2   3   4   5   6   7   8   9   10

DISCONNECTED   CONNECTED

MEANINGFUL COINCIDENCES, THEMES, OR PATTERNS I ENCOUNTERED TODAY:

_____

_____

_____

INTUITIVE INSIGHTS I EXPERIENCED INTERNALLY OR PHYSICALLY:

_____

_____

THINGS THAT CONNECTED ME TO MY INTUITION TODAY:

☐ GETTING QUALITY QUIET TIME OR TIME ALONE

☐ MINDFULLY SLOWING DOWN

☐ LOWERING MY STRESS LEVELS

☐ HAVING NOURISHING WORK AND HOME ROUTINES

☐ KEEPING MY ENVIRONMENT TIDY AND INVITING

☐ LISTENING TO SOFT MUSIC OR NATURE SOUNDS

☐ PULLING AN ORACLE CARD FOR INSPIRATION

☐ OTHER:_____

WHERE/WHEN DID I FEEL MOST INTUITIVE TODAY?

_____

_____

WHAT WAS MOST ENCOURAGING, COMFORTING, OR EXCITING ABOUT
CONNECTING WITH MY INTUITION TODAY?

_____

_____

MORNING REFLECTION   DATE ___/___/___

HOW I'D RATE MY OPENNESS TO INTUITIVE GUIDANCE TODAY:

1   2   3   4   5   6   7   8   9   10

CLOSED/DISTRACTED   OPEN/GROUNDED

LAST NIGHT'S INTUITIVE DREAMS, OR INTUITIVE INSIGHTS WHEN I AWOKE:

_____

_____

TODAY I'D LIKE TO RECEIVE AN INTUITIVE SIGN ABOUT:

_____

_____

GOALS TO HELP ME FEEL LESS SCATTERED AND MORE CENTERED TODAY:

_____   _____

_____   _____

HOW I PLAN TO CONNECT MINDFULLY WITH MY INTUITION TODAY:

_____

_____

_____

MY MORNING INTUITIVE ROUTINE INCLUDED:

☐ MEDITATION   ☐ TIME IN NATURE   ☐ SELF-CARE:_____
☐ PRAYER   ☐ A HEALTHY BREAKFAST   ☐ OTHER:_____
☐ JOURNALING   ☐ SACRED PAUSES   _____

GUT CHECK—WHAT IS THE STRONGEST INSTINCT I HAVE RIGHT NOW ABOUT
HOW TO APPROACH A SITUATION, PERSON, OR ISSUE I'M FACING TODAY?

_____

_____

_____

EVENING REFLECTION

MEANINGFUL COINCIDENCES, THEMES, OR PATTERNS I ENCOUNTERED TODAY:

_____

_____

_____

INTUITIVE INSIGHTS I EXPERIENCED INTERNALLY OR PHYSICALLY:

_____

_____

THINGS THAT CONNECTED ME TO MY INTUITION TODAY:

☐ GETTING QUALITY QUIET TIME OR TIME ALONE

☐ MINDFULLY SLOWING DOWN

☐ LOWERING MY STRESS LEVELS

☐ HAVING NOURISHING WORK AND HOME ROUTINES

☐ KEEPING MY ENVIRONMENT TIDY AND INVITING

☐ LISTENING TO SOFT MUSIC OR NATURE SOUNDS

☐ PULLING AN ORACLE CARD FOR INSPIRATION

☐ OTHER:_____

WHERE/WHEN DID I FEEL MOST INTUITIVE TODAY?

_____

_____

WHAT WAS MOST ENCOURAGING, COMFORTING, OR EXCITING ABOUT
CONNECTING WITH MY INTUITION TODAY?

_____

_____

MORNING REFLECTION   DATE ___/___/___

HOW I'D RATE MY OPENNESS TO INTUITIVE GUIDANCE TODAY:

1   2   3   4   5   6   7   8   9   10

CLOSED/DISTRACTED   OPEN/GROUNDED

LAST NIGHT'S INTUITIVE DREAMS, OR INTUITIVE INSIGHTS WHEN I AWOKE:

_____

_____

TODAY I'D LIKE TO RECEIVE AN INTUITIVE SIGN ABOUT:

_____

_____

GOALS TO HELP ME FEEL LESS SCATTERED AND MORE CENTERED TODAY:

_____   _____

_____   _____

HOW I PLAN TO CONNECT MINDFULLY WITH MY INTUITION TODAY:

_____

_____

_____

MY MORNING INTUITIVE ROUTINE INCLUDED:.

☐ MEDITATION   ☐ TIME IN NATURE   ☐ SELF-CARE:_____

☐ PRAYER   ☐ A HEALTHY BREAKFAST   ☐ OTHER:_____

☐ JOURNALING   ☐ SACRED PAUSES   _____

GUT CHECK—WHAT IS THE STRONGEST INSTINCT I HAVE RIGHT NOW ABOUT
HOW TO APPROACH A SITUATION, PERSON, OR ISSUE I'M FACING TODAY?

_____

_____

EVENING REFLECTION

HOW I'D RATE MY ABILITY TO CONNECT WITH MY INTUITION TODAY:

1   2   3   4   5   6   7   8   9   10

DISCONNECTED   CONNECTED

MEANINGFUL COINCIDENCES, THEMES, OR PATTERNS I ENCOUNTERED TODAY:

_____

_____

_____

INTUITIVE INSIGHTS I EXPERIENCED INTERNALLY OR PHYSICALLY:

_____

_____

THINGS THAT CONNECTED ME TO MY INTUITION TODAY:

☐ GETTING QUALITY QUIET TIME OR TIME ALONE

☐ MINDFULLY SLOWING DOWN

☐ LOWERING MY STRESS LEVELS

☐ HAVING NOURISHING WORK AND HOME ROUTINES

☐ KEEPING MY ENVIRONMENT TIDY AND INVITING

☐ LISTENING TO SOFT MUSIC OR NATURE SOUNDS

☐ PULLING AN ORACLE CARD FOR INSPIRATION

☐ OTHER:_____

WHERE/WHEN DID I FEEL MOST INTUITIVE TODAY?

_____

_____

WHAT WAS MOST ENCOURAGING, COMFORTING, OR EXCITING ABOUT CONNECTING WITH MY INTUITION TODAY?

_____

_____

MORNING REFLECTION DATE ___/___/___

HOW I'D RATE MY OPENNESS TO INTUITIVE GUIDANCE TODAY:

1   2   3.   4   5   6   7   8   9   10

CLOSED/DISTRACTED   OPEN/GROUNDED

LAST NIGHT'S INTUITIVE DREAMS, OR INTUITIVE INSIGHTS WHEN I AWOKE:

_____

_____

TODAY I'D LIKE TO RECEIVE AN INTUITIVE SIGN ABOUT:

_____

_____

GOALS TO HELP ME FEEL LESS SCATTERED AND MORE CENTERED TODAY:

_____   _____

_____   _____

HOW I PLAN TO CONNECT MINDFULLY WITH MY INTUITION TODAY:

_____

_____

_____

MY MORNING INTUITIVE ROUTINE INCLUDED:

☐ MEDITATION   ☐ TIME IN NATURE   ☐ SELF-CARE:_____

☐ PRAYER   ☐ A HEALTHY BREAKFAST   ☐ OTHER:_____

☐ JOURNALING   ☐ SACRED PAUSES   _____

GUT CHECK—WHAT IS THE STRONGEST INSTINCT I HAVE RIGHT NOW ABOUT
HOW TO APPROACH A SITUATION, PERSON, OR ISSUE I'M FACING TODAY?

_____

_____

_____

EVENING REFLECTION

HOW I'D RATE MY ABILITY TO CONNECT WITH MY INTUITION TODAY:

1   2   3   4   5   6   7   8   9   10

DISCONNECTED   CONNECTED

MEANINGFUL COINCIDENCES, THEMES, OR PATTERNS I ENCOUNTERED TODAY:

_____

_____

_____

INTUITIVE INSIGHTS I EXPERIENCED INTERNALLY OR PHYSICALLY:

_____

_____

THINGS THAT CONNECTED ME TO MY INTUITION TODAY:

☐ GETTING QUALITY QUIET TIME OR TIME ALONE

☐ MINDFULLY SLOWING DOWN

☐ LOWERING MY STRESS LEVELS

☐ HAVING NOURISHING WORK AND HOME ROUTINES

☐ KEEPING MY ENVIRONMENT TIDY AND INVITING

☐ LISTENING TO SOFT MUSIC OR NATURE SOUNDS

☐ PULLING AN ORACLE CARD FOR INSPIRATION

☐ OTHER:_____

WHERE/WHEN DID I FEEL MOST INTUITIVE TODAY?

_____

_____

WHAT WAS MOST ENCOURAGING, COMFORTING, OR EXCITING ABOUT
CONNECTING WITH MY INTUITION TODAY?

_____

_____

MORNING REFLECTION

DATE ___ / ___ / ___

LAST NIGHT'S INTUITIVE DREAMS, OR INTUITIVE INSIGHTS WHEN I AWOKE:
_____
_____

TODAY I'D LIKE TO RECEIVE AN INTUITIVE SIGN ABOUT:
_____
_____

GOALS TO HELP ME FEEL LESS SCATTERED AND MORE CENTERED TODAY:
_____   _____
_____   _____

HOW I PLAN TO CONNECT MINDFULLY WITH MY INTUITION TODAY:
_____
_____
_____

MY MORNING INTUITIVE ROUTINE INCLUDED:

☐ MEDITATION   ☐ TIME IN NATURE   ☐ SELF-CARE:_____
☐ PRAYER   ☐ A HEALTHY BREAKFAST   ☐ OTHER:_____
☐ JOURNALING   ☐ SACRED PAUSES   _____

GUT CHECK—WHAT IS THE STRONGEST INSTINCT I HAVE RIGHT NOW ABOUT
HOW TO APPROACH A SITUATION, PERSON, OR ISSUE I'M FACING TODAY?
_____
_____
_____

EVENING REFLECTION

HOW I'D RATE MY ABILITY TO CONNECT WITH MY INTUITION TODAY:

1   2   3   4   5   6   7   8   9   10

DISCONNECTED   CONNECTED

MEANINGFUL COINCIDENCES, THEMES, OR PATTERNS I ENCOUNTERED TODAY:

_____

_____

_____

INTUITIVE INSIGHTS I EXPERIENCED INTERNALLY OR PHYSICALLY:

_____

_____

THINGS THAT CONNECTED ME TO MY INTUITION TODAY:

☐ GETTING QUALITY QUIET TIME OR TIME ALONE

☐ MINDFULLY SLOWING DOWN

☐ LOWERING MY STRESS LEVELS

☐ HAVING NOURISHING WORK AND HOME ROUTINES

☐ KEEPING MY ENVIRONMENT TIDY AND INVITING

☐ LISTENING TO SOFT MUSIC OR NATURE SOUNDS

☐ PULLING AN ORACLE CARD FOR INSPIRATION

☐ OTHER:_____

WHERE/WHEN DID I FEEL MOST INTUITIVE TODAY?

_____

_____

WHAT WAS MOST ENCOURAGING, COMFORTING, OR EXCITING ABOUT
CONNECTING WITH MY INTUITION TODAY?

_____

_____

MORNING REFLECTION   DATE ___/___/___

HOW I'D RATE MY OPENNESS TO INTUITIVE GUIDANCE TODAY:

1   2   3   4   5   6   7   8   9   10

CLOSED/DISTRACTED   OPEN/GROUNDED

LAST NIGHT'S INTUITIVE DREAMS, OR INTUITIVE INSIGHTS WHEN I AWOKE:

_____

_____

TODAY I'D LIKE TO RECEIVE AN INTUITIVE SIGN ABOUT:

_____

_____

GOALS TO HELP ME FEEL LESS SCATTERED AND MORE CENTERED TODAY:

_____   _____

_____   _____

HOW I PLAN TO CONNECT MINDFULLY WITH MY INTUITION TODAY:

_____

_____

_____

MY MORNING INTUITIVE ROUTINE INCLUDED:

- ☐ MEDITATION
- ☐ PRAYER
- ☐ JOURNALING

- ☐ TIME IN NATURE
- ☐ A HEALTHY BREAKFAST
- ☐ SACRED PAUSES

- ☐ SELF-CARE:_____
- ☐ OTHER:_____
- _____

GUT CHECK—WHAT IS THE STRONGEST INSTINCT I HAVE RIGHT NOW ABOUT
HOW TO APPROACH A SITUATION, PERSON, OR ISSUE I'M FACING TODAY?

_____

_____

_____

EVENING REFLECTION

HOW I'D RATE MY ABILITY TO CONNECT WITH MY INTUITION TODAY:

1	2	3	4	5	6	7	8	9	10

DISCONNECTED   CONNECTED

MEANINGFUL COINCIDENCES, THEMES, OR PATTERNS I ENCOUNTERED TODAY:

_____

_____

_____

INTUITIVE INSIGHTS I EXPERIENCED INTERNALLY OR PHYSICALLY:

_____

_____

THINGS THAT CONNECTED ME TO MY INTUITION TODAY:

☐ GETTING QUALITY QUIET TIME OR TIME ALONE

☐ MINDFULLY SLOWING DOWN

☐ LOWERING MY STRESS LEVELS

☐ HAVING NOURISHING WORK AND HOME ROUTINES

☐ KEEPING MY ENVIRONMENT TIDY AND INVITING

☐ LISTENING TO SOFT MUSIC OR NATURE SOUNDS

☐ PULLING AN ORACLE CARD FOR INSPIRATION

☐ OTHER:_____

WHERE/WHEN DID I FEEL MOST INTUITIVE TODAY?

_____

_____

WHAT WAS MOST ENCOURAGING, COMFORTING, OR EXCITING ABOUT
CONNECTING WITH MY INTUITION TODAY?

_____

_____

MORNING REFLECTION

DATE ___ / ___ / ___

HOW I'D RATE MY OPENNESS TO INTUITIVE GUIDANCE TODAY:

1   2   3   4   5   6   7   8   9   10

CLOSED/DISTRACTED   OPEN/GROUNDED

LAST NIGHT'S INTUITIVE DREAMS, OR INTUITIVE INSIGHTS WHEN I AWOKE:

_____

_____

TODAY I'D LIKE TO RECEIVE AN INTUITIVE SIGN ABOUT:

_____

_____

GOALS TO HELP ME FEEL LESS SCATTERED AND MORE CENTERED TODAY:

_____   _____

_____   _____

HOW I PLAN TO CONNECT MINDFULLY WITH MY INTUITION TODAY:

_____

_____

_____

MY MORNING INTUITIVE ROUTINE INCLUDED:

☐ MEDITATION   ☐ TIME IN NATURE   ☐ SELF-CARE:_____

☐ PRAYER   ☐ A HEALTHY BREAKFAST   ☐ OTHER:_____

☐ JOURNALING   ☐ SACRED PAUSES   _____

GUT CHECK—WHAT IS THE STRONGEST INSTINCT I HAVE RIGHT NOW ABOUT
HOW TO APPROACH A SITUATION, PERSON, OR ISSUE I'M FACING TODAY?

_____

_____

_____

EVENING REFLECTION

HOW I'D RATE MY ABILITY TO CONNECT WITH MY INTUITION TODAY:

1   2   3   4   5   6   7   8   9   10

DISCONNECTED   CONNECTED

MEANINGFUL COINCIDENCES, THEMES, OR PATTERNS I ENCOUNTERED TODAY:

_____

_____

_____

INTUITIVE INSIGHTS I EXPERIENCED INTERNALLY OR PHYSICALLY:

_____

_____

THINGS THAT CONNECTED ME TO MY INTUITION TODAY:

☐ GETTING QUALITY QUIET TIME OR TIME ALONE

☐ MINDFULLY SLOWING DOWN

☐ LOWERING MY STRESS LEVELS

☐ HAVING NOURISHING WORK AND HOME ROUTINES

☐ KEEPING MY ENVIRONMENT TIDY AND INVITING

☐ LISTENING TO SOFT MUSIC OR NATURE SOUNDS

☐ PULLING AN ORACLE CARD FOR INSPIRATION

☐ OTHER:_____

WHERE/WHEN DID I FEEL MOST INTUITIVE TODAY?

_____

WHAT WAS MOST ENCOURAGING, COMFORTING, OR EXCITING ABOUT
CONNECTING WITH MY INTUITION TODAY?

_____

_____

MORNING REFLECTION

DATE ___/___/___

HOW I'D RATE MY OPENNESS TO INTUITIVE GUIDANCE TODAY:

1   2   3   4   5   6   7   8   9   10

CLOSED/DISTRACTED   OPEN/GROUNDED

LAST NIGHT'S INTUITIVE DREAMS, OR INTUITIVE INSIGHTS WHEN I AWOKE:

_____

_____

TODAY I'D LIKE TO RECEIVE AN INTUITIVE SIGN ABOUT:

_____

_____

GOALS TO HELP ME FEEL LESS SCATTERED AND MORE CENTERED TODAY:

_____   _____

_____   _____

HOW I PLAN TO CONNECT MINDFULLY WITH MY INTUITION TODAY:

_____

_____

_____

MY MORNING INTUITIVE ROUTINE INCLUDED:

☐ MEDITATION   ☐ TIME IN NATURE   ☐ SELF-CARE:_____

☐ PRAYER   ☐ A HEALTHY BREAKFAST   ☐ OTHER:_____

☐ JOURNALING   ☐ SACRED PAUSES   _____

GUT CHECK—WHAT IS THE STRONGEST INSTINCT I HAVE RIGHT NOW ABOUT
HOW TO APPROACH A SITUATION, PERSON, OR ISSUE I'M FACING TODAY?

_____

_____

_____

EVENING REFLECTION

HOW I'D RATE MY ABILITY TO CONNECT WITH MY INTUITION TODAY:

1   2   3   4   5   6   7   8   9   10

DISCONNECTED   CONNECTED

MEANINGFUL COINCIDENCES, THEMES, OR PATTERNS I ENCOUNTERED TODAY:

_____

_____

_____

INTUITIVE INSIGHTS I EXPERIENCED INTERNALLY OR PHYSICALLY:

_____

_____

THINGS THAT CONNECTED ME TO MY INTUITION TODAY:

☐ GETTING QUALITY QUIET TIME OR TIME ALONE

☐ MINDFULLY SLOWING DOWN

☐ LOWERING MY STRESS LEVELS

☐ HAVING NOURISHING WORK AND HOME ROUTINES

☐ KEEPING MY ENVIRONMENT TIDY AND INVITING

☐ LISTENING TO SOFT MUSIC OR NATURE SOUNDS

☐ PULLING AN ORACLE CARD FOR INSPIRATION

☐ OTHER:_____

WHERE/WHEN DID I FEEL MOST INTUITIVE TODAY?

_____

_____

WHAT WAS MOST ENCOURAGING, COMFORTING, OR EXCITING ABOUT
CONNECTING WITH MY INTUITION TODAY?

_____

_____

MORNING REFLECTION

DATE ___/___/___

LAST NIGHT'S INTUITIVE DREAMS, OR INTUITIVE INSIGHTS WHEN I AWOKE:

_____

_____

TODAY I'D LIKE TO RECEIVE AN INTUITIVE SIGN ABOUT:

_____

_____

GOALS TO HELP ME FEEL LESS SCATTERED AND MORE CENTERED TODAY:

_____   _____

_____   _____

HOW I PLAN TO CONNECT MINDFULLY WITH MY INTUITION TODAY:

_____

_____

_____

MY MORNING INTUITIVE ROUTINE INCLUDED:

☐ MEDITATION   ☐ TIME IN NATURE   ☐ SELF-CARE:_____

☐ PRAYER   ☐ A HEALTHY BREAKFAST   ☐ OTHER:_____

☐ JOURNALING   ☐ SACRED PAUSES   _____

GUT CHECK—WHAT IS THE STRONGEST INSTINCT I HAVE RIGHT NOW ABOUT
HOW TO APPROACH A SITUATION, PERSON, OR ISSUE I'M FACING TODAY?

_____

_____

_____

EVENING REFLECTION

HOW I'D RATE MY ABILITY TO CONNECT WITH MY INTUITION TODAY:

1   2   3   4   5   6   7   8   9   10

DISCONNECTED   CONNECTED

MEANINGFUL COINCIDENCES, THEMES, OR PATTERNS I ENCOUNTERED TODAY:

_____

_____

_____

INTUITIVE INSIGHTS I EXPERIENCED INTERNALLY OR PHYSICALLY:

_____

_____

THINGS THAT CONNECTED ME TO MY INTUITION TODAY:

☐ GETTING QUALITY QUIET TIME OR TIME ALONE

☐ MINDFULLY SLOWING DOWN

☐ LOWERING MY STRESS LEVELS

☐ HAVING NOURISHING WORK AND HOME ROUTINES

☐ KEEPING MY ENVIRONMENT TIDY AND INVITING

☐ LISTENING TO SOFT MUSIC OR NATURE SOUNDS

☐ PULLING AN ORACLE CARD FOR INSPIRATION

☐ OTHER:_____

WHERE/WHEN DID I FEEL MOST INTUITIVE TODAY?

_____

_____

WHAT WAS MOST ENCOURAGING, COMFORTING, OR EXCITING ABOUT CONNECTING WITH MY INTUITION TODAY?

_____

_____

MORNING REFLECTION   DATE ___ / ___ / ___

HOW I'D RATE MY OPENNESS TO INTUITIVE GUIDANCE TODAY:

1   2   3   4   5   6   7   8   9   10

CLOSED/DISTRACTED   OPEN/GROUNDED

LAST NIGHT'S INTUITIVE DREAMS, OR INTUITIVE INSIGHTS WHEN I AWOKE:

_____

_____

TODAY I'D LIKE TO RECEIVE AN INTUITIVE SIGN ABOUT:

_____

_____

GOALS TO HELP ME FEEL LESS SCATTERED AND MORE CENTERED TODAY:

_____   _____

_____   _____

HOW I PLAN TO CONNECT MINDFULLY WITH MY INTUITION TODAY:

_____

_____

_____

MY MORNING INTUITIVE ROUTINE INCLUDED:

☐ MEDITATION   ☐ TIME IN NATURE   ☐ SELF-CARE:_____

☐ PRAYER   ☐ A HEALTHY BREAKFAST   ☐ OTHER:_____

☐ JOURNALING   ☐ SACRED PAUSES   _____

GUT CHECK—WHAT IS THE STRONGEST INSTINCT I HAVE RIGHT NOW ABOUT
HOW TO APPROACH A SITUATION, PERSON, OR ISSUE I'M FACING TODAY?

_____

_____

_____

EVENING REFLECTION

HOW I'D RATE MY ABILITY TO CONNECT WITH MY INTUITION TODAY:

| 1 | 2 | 3 | 4 | 5 | 6 | 7 | 8 | 9 | 10 |

DISCONNECTED   CONNECTED

MEANINGFUL COINCIDENCES, THEMES, OR PATTERNS I ENCOUNTERED TODAY:

_____

_____

_____

INTUITIVE INSIGHTS I EXPERIENCED INTERNALLY OR PHYSICALLY:

_____

_____

THINGS THAT CONNECTED ME TO MY INTUITION TODAY:

☐ GETTING QUALITY QUIET TIME OR TIME ALONE

☐ MINDFULLY SLOWING DOWN

☐ LOWERING MY STRESS LEVELS

☐ HAVING NOURISHING WORK AND HOME ROUTINES

☐ KEEPING MY ENVIRONMENT TIDY AND INVITING

☐ LISTENING TO SOFT MUSIC OR NATURE SOUNDS

☐ PULLING AN ORACLE CARD FOR INSPIRATION

☐ OTHER:_____

WHERE/WHEN DID I FEEL MOST INTUITIVE TODAY?

_____

_____

WHAT WAS MOST ENCOURAGING, COMFORTING, OR EXCITING ABOUT
CONNECTING WITH MY INTUITION TODAY?

_____

_____

INSIGHTS

A Mandala Journal

MANDALA
PUBLISHING

www.mandalaearth.com

Art Direction by Ashley Quackenbush
Design by Stephanie Odeh

Written by Tanya Carroll Richardson, author of
Awakening Intuition: Oracle Deck and Guidebook